THE AUTHOR OF WAVERLEY

The Author of Waverley

A Critical Study of Walter Scott

D. D. DEVLIN

LEWISBURG: BUCKNELL UNIVERSITY PRESS

© D. D. Devlin 1971

Library of Congress Catalogue
Card Number: 71–146129
First American Edition 1971
Associated University Presses
Cranbury, New Jersey 08512
ISBN: 0–8387–7925–5

Printed in Great Britain

Contents

	Preface	7
1	Scott and Fiction	11
2	Scott and History	34
3	*Waverley*	56
4	*A Legend of Montrose* and *Rob Roy*	81
5	*The Bride of Lammermoor*	99
6	*Redgauntlet*	114
	Index	141

TO EDITH

Preface

I HAVE not attempted a critical discussion and assessment of every Scott novel. I do not insist that the five novels I have chosen for detailed analysis — *Waverley*, *A Legend of Montrose*, *Rob Roy*, *The Bride of Lammermoor*, *Redgauntlet* — are Scott's best work. (Any list of the best Scott novels would include, for example, *Old Mortality*, *The Abbott*, *The Heart of Midlothian* and *The Fair Maid of Perth*.) I have chosen to discuss them because they illustrate best the two aspects of Scott's fiction I wished to describe and emphasise: the nature of his concern with the past and the relation of his comic characters to the structure of the novels. And it is the coherence and structure of the novels I want to insist upon: a structure that springs from and reinforces his intense interest in man in history and his huge enjoyment of people.

D. D. DEVLIN

Acknowledgements

Chapter 4, '*A Legend of Montrose* and *Rob Roy*', originally appeared under the title 'Character and Narrative in Scott: *A Legend of Montrose* and *Rob Roy*', in *Essays in Criticism*, vol. xviii, no. 2 (April 1968). Chapter 6, '*Redgauntlet*', originally appeared in *A Review of English Literature*, vol. iv, no. 1 (1963).

1 Scott and Fiction

His works possess the rare and invaluable property of
originality, to which all other qualities are as dust in the
balance. (SCOTT)

I

SCOTT was a gentle and casual critic; the gentleness came
from his generosity and good-nature, the casualness from
his conviction that there were more important things than
literature in general and fiction in particular. This conviction has been his undoing. 'I need hardly repeat', writes
Lockhart, 'that Scott never considered any amount of
literary distinction as entitled to be spoken of in the same
breath with mastery in the higher departments of practical
life . . . To have done things worthy to be written, was in
his eyes a dignity to which no man made any approach
who had only written things worthy to be read.'[1] When
the modern reader comes on this, or reads Scott's answer
to the complaint that the first three volumes of *The Heart
of Midlothian* were good but the fourth bad – 'Authors
should be reasonably well pleased when three-fourths of
their work are acceptable to the reader' – he loses patience,
and attributes to vanity or flippancy or false gentility
Scott's refusal to take seriously fiction or the criticism of
fiction. But Scott's attitude has a different origin: it comes
from a steady pessimism which colours everything he
wrote and which insists that any high notions of the moral
power of literature imply an impossible belief in man's
ability to improve or to change. Scott's favourite poem

was 'The Vanity of Human Wishes' and behind him there is always Dr Johnson.

Yet Scott wrote extensively about fiction. His essays on earlier novelists, the introductory matter of his own novels, his *Letters* and his *Journal* provide a body of perceptive comment on fiction. He does not give a consistent view of fiction or a sustained examination of novels or the problems of the novelist. Instead, Scott talks for the most part about those novelists and aspects of fiction which interest him and which have some relevance to his own practice as a novelist; and his comments on what other novelists do or fail to do provide a series of hints and glimpses into his own interests and intentions as a writer.

But only hints. What most impressed contemporary readers of the Waverley novels was their originality; Scott was doing something in fiction that had never been done before. Jeffrey's review of *Waverley* insists that it is not only 'incomparably superior to anything of the sort which has been offered to the public for the last sixty years', but is different in kind, wholly original: 'The secret of this success, we take it, is merely that the author is a person of genius.' And today, in spite of Scott's disclaimers, in spite of his endlessly generous tributes to other writers, it is his originality, the newness of what he did, that becomes more and more striking. He is an 'individual talent' only slightly related to any tradition. (The opening chapter of *Waverley* contains a rejection of several types of contemporary fiction.) Scott warns against seeing influence or even plagiarism where none exists, and quarrels with

> critics who conceive they detect a plagiarist whenever they see a resemblance in the general subject of a work, to one which has been treated before by an inferior artist. It is a favourite theme of laborious dulness, to trace out such coincidences; because they

appear to reduce genius of the higher order to the usual standard of humanity, and, of course, to bring the author nearer a level with his critics.[2]

In the next chapter I want to consider the nature of Scott's historical fiction. In this chapter I want to see what understanding of his work can be gained from what he has said about 'the novelist's art' (the phrase is Scott's), about other novelists and about the aims and some of the problems of fiction.

II

'I am, I own, no great believer in the moral utility to be derived from fictitious compositions,' wrote Scott; but if he has no high hopes he has no gloomy fears and finds that 'the worst evil to be apprehended from the perusal of novels is, that the habit is apt to generate an indisposition to real history and useful literature'. This sobriety has the advantage that it enables Scott to say that 'the professed moral of a piece is usually what the reader is least interested in'. And even if at the end of his book (Scott is thinking of Richardson's *Pamela*) the novelist represents virtue as triumphant, the 'direct and obvious' moral that is drawn from the narrative will have much less effect on the reader than 'the mode in which the story is treated in the course of its details'.

> In fact it is not passages of ludicrous indelicacy that corrupt the manners of a people — it is the sonnets which a prurient genius like Master Little sings *virginibus puerisque* — it is the sentimental slang, half lewd, half methodistic that debauches the understanding, inflames the sleeping passions and prepares the reader to give way as soon as a tempter appears.[3]

For Scott the real moral value of literature is that it extends our sympathies and enlarges our respect for people. *The*

Vicar of Wakefield is praised because Goldsmith 'contrives so well to reconcile us to human nature'. An author who does this can be excused anything, for this will be the effective moral of his work. Scott writes of *Tristram Shandy*:

> Uncle Toby and his faithful squire, the most delightful characters in the work, or perhaps in any other, are drawm with such a pleasing force and discrimination, that they more than entitle the author to a free pardon for his literacy peculations, his indecorum, and his affectation; nay authorize him to leave the court of criticism not forgiven only, but applauded and rewarded as one who has exalted and honoured humanity . . .[4]

It is this celebration of human nature by the novelist which justifies his work and gives the greatest pleasure and the greatest consolation. The prose and the sentiment echo Johnson when Scott says of novels:

> but in truth, when we consider how many hours of languor and anxiety, of deserted age and solitary celibacy, of pain even and poverty, are beguiled by the perusal of these light volumes, we cannot austerely condemn the source from which is drawn the alleviation of such a portion of human misery, or consider the regulation of this department as beneath the sober consideration of the critic.[5]

III

Scott distinguishes between the Romance and the Novel. In Romance the interest 'turns upon marvellous and uncommon incidents'; in a novel 'the events are accommodated in the ordinary train of human events, and the modern state of society'. Scott's only total failure – *The Monastery* – is the one narrative which turns upon 'marvellous incidents'. It is a dull book, and Scott finds that Romances are duller than Novels. He refers to the popularity in England at the end of the seventeenth century of the Romances of Calprenède and Scudéry and finds them monotonous, unimaginative and full of 'unnatural metaphysical jargon, sentimental languor and flat love-intrigue'. The reason for their popularity was simple: 'there was nothing better to supply their room' until they were superseded by Le Sage, Richardson, Fielding and Smollett, who provided for the first time 'variety of character, just traits of feeling, acute views of life'. And for all his generosity Scott thinks little of romance writers like Mrs Radcliffe. In his comments on Mrs Radcliffe he implies a view of the novel which helps to explain his own practice and power.

The species of romance which Mrs Radcliffe introduced, bears nearly the same relation to the novel that the modern anomaly entitled a melodrame does to the proper drama. It does not appeal to the judgment by deep delineations of human feeling, or stir the passions by scenes of deep pathos, or awaken the fancy by tracing out, with spirit and vivacity, the lighter marks of life and manners, or excite mirth by strong representations of the ludicrous or humorous. In other words, it attains its interest neither by the path of comedy nor of tragedy; and yet it has, notwithstanding, a deep, decided, and powerful effect, gained by means independent of both — by an appeal, in one word, to the passion of fear, whether excited by natural dangers, or by the suggestions of superstition. The force, therefore, of the production, lies in the delineation of external incident, while the characters of the agents, like the figures in many landscapes, are entirely subordinate to the scenes in which they are placed; and are only distinguished by such outlines as make them seem appropriate to the rocks and trees, which have been the artist's principal objects. The persons introduced — and here also the correspondence holds betwixt the melodrame and the romantic novel — bear the features, not of individuals, but of the class to which they belong. A dark and tyrannical count; an aged crone of a housekeeper, the depositary of many a family legend; a garrulous waiting-maid; a gay and light-hearted valet; a villain or two of all work; and a heroine, fulfilled with all perfections, and subjected to all manner of hazards, form the stock-in-trade of a romancer or a melo-dramatist; and if these personages be dressed in the proper costume, and converse in language sufficiently appropriate to their stations and qualities, it is not expected that the audience shall shake their sides at the humour of the dialogue, or weep over its pathos.[6]

The general indictment is then focused on Mrs Radcliffe, and Scott finds that she 'has neither displayed the command of the human passions, nor the insight into the human heart, nor the observation of life and manners', which are the signs of a great novelist. She does not give us the truth about either the interior or exterior life; she 'rather walks in fairy-land than in the region of realities'. It is knowledge and skill in drawing character and the passions that for Scott always count most. When he finds that the same four great talents are necessary for success in writing either plays or novels it is 'force of character' he mentions first and 'a well-constructed plot' which he mentions last.

A weakness of Scott's comments on fiction is the inadequacy of his critical terms; a sign of his critical intelligence is his sense of their inadequacy in describing his own work. He talks of character and plot; he knows there is an 'art of the novel', but sees this art as the creation of a structure which is indistinguishable from plot. And yet his comments on plot and plot-construction are often uneasy; he is half aware that there can be another and better structure in a novel, a structure which he established in the Waverley novels and which is an internal principle of organisation that works through theme and character.

It is in his comments on the relationship between

character and plot that Scott is most unsatisfactory and tantalising. ('Plot', 'narrative' and 'story' are for Scott interchangeable terms.) He sees plot as largely a skilful contrivance on the part of the novelist. He knows he is not expert at this particular technique, and what he most admires in other novelists and sees as his own strength is skill in character drawing. We are tantalised because we can now see that the best Waverley novels have a structure or shape as clear as Scott's favourite *Tom Jones*; we can see, however, that this has little to do with the plot, but with the characters. Scott's unease with his own discussions of the importance and relationship of character and plot comes out in a number of ways. Smollett is blamed because in his novels 'characters are introduced and dropped without scruple, and, at the end of the work, the hero is found surrounded by a very different set of associates from those with which his fortnue seemed at first indissolubly connected'.[7] Richardson is praised because every character that is introduced does something to further the plot. Writing of the novels of Robert Bage, Scott says approvingly that

> the mere story of the novels seldom possesses much interest – it is the conduct of his personages as thinking and speaking beings in which we are interested; and contrary to the general case, the reader is seldom or never tempted to pass over the dialogue in order to continue the narrative.[8]

Writing of *Waverley*, Scott said that he felt that the success of the book 'was to depend upon the characters more than upon the story'; and in the Advertisement to *The Antiquary* (1816), when Scott thought that he had come to the end of his career as a novelist after three novels, he insisted that he had been 'more solicitous to describe manners minutely than to arrange in any care an artificial and combined narrative, and have but to regret that I felt myself unable to unite these two requisites of a good Novel'. A few lines later he adds with excessive modesty that his novels 'have little more than some truth of colouring to recommend them'.

The most interesting of all Scott's comments, for its mixture of insight and blindness, is in the Introductory Epistle to *The Fortunes of Nigel* (1822), where Captain Clutterbuck and the Author of Waverley have a conversation about fiction. (The dialogue contains some of the remarks which critics have long held against Scott – 'I care not who knows it – I write for general amusement'. Too seldom quoted is the next part of this sentence: '. . . and though I never will aim at popularity by what I think unworthy means, I will not, on the other hand be pertinacious in the defence of my own errors against the voice of the public.' That Scott did *not* write for general amusement will be clear to anyone who reads even two or three pages of his *Journal*.) Captain Clutterbuck says that the Author of Waverley writes the novels too quickly and asks that he should 'take time at least to arrange [the] story'. Scott answers:

Author. Believe me, I have not been fool enough to neglect ordinary precautions. I have repeatedly laid down my future work to scale, divided it into volumes and chapters, and endeavoured to construct a story which I meant should evolve itself gradually and strikingly, maintain suspense, and stimulate curiosity; and which, finally, should terminate in a striking catastrophe. But I think there is a demon who seats himself on the feather of my pen when I begin to write, and leads it astray from the purpose. Characters expand under my hand; incidents are multiplied; the story lingers, while the materials increase; my regular mansion turns out a Gothic anomaly, and the work is closed long before I have attained the point I proposed.

Captain. Resolution and determined forbearance might remedy that evil.

Author. Alas! my dear sir, you do not know the force of
paternal affection. When I light on such a character as Bailie
Jarvie, or Dalgetty, my imagination brightens, and my conception becomes clearer at every step which I take in his company,
although it leads me many a weary mile away from the regular
road, and forces me to leap hedge and ditch to get back into the
route again. If I resist the temptation, as you advise me, my
thoughts become prosy, flat, and dull; I write painfully to myself, and under a consciousness of flagging which makes me flag
still more; the sunshine with which fancy had invested the
incidents departs from them, and leaves everything dull and
gloomy.

There is a 'plot' or 'story', which alone can provide the
structure of a novel and make it a 'regular mansion'; and
there is 'character', which regularly leads him away from
the regular road. It is remarkable that Scott does not see
that the essential narrative structure of his novels is one
of character; that, for example, Nicol Jarvie and Dalgetty
and Cuddie Headrigg are the means by which we grasp
the total story or meaning of *Rob Roy*, *A Legend of Montrose* and *Old Mortality*.

Scott's emphasis on character and his interest in the
sort of unity a novel may have which does not depend on
plot appear many times in his essays on novelists. In his
essay on Le Sage, Scott says of the *Diable Boiteux* that
'There is no book in existence in which so much of the
human character, under all its various shades and phases is
described in so few words.'[9] And in a comment on the
same writer's *Gil Blas* Scott seems to be describing his
own practice in *Waverley*: 'Gil Blas is the principal character in the moving scene, where, though he frequently
plays a subordinate part in the action, all that he lays
before us is coloured with his own opinions, remarks and
sensations.'[10] However true of *Waverley*, the words even
more aptly describe Mackenzie's *The Man of Feeling*

(1771). Scott thought highly of Mackenzie and dedicated *Waverley* to him. He sees Mackenzie as possessing, supremely, originality (the motto at the head of this chapter refers to Mackenzie), and his originality and achievement lie in his reaching and sustaining

> a tone of moral pathos, by representing the effect of incidents, whether important or trifling, upon the human mind, and especially on those which were not only just, honourable, and intelligent, but so framed as to be responsive to those finer feelings to which ordinary hearts are callous.

His novels are 'rather the history of effects produced on the human mind by a series of events, than the narrative of the events themselves'. He and Sterne belong to the same class, and if Sterne is more brilliant, Mackenzie is superior in his 'accuracy of human feeling'.[11] Scott, however, does not find the picaresque novel satisfactory, even at its best in *Gil Blas* or *Roderick Random*; in such novels characters appear and reappear 'without, perhaps, having any permanent influence on the progress of the story'. The end comes only because 'every story must have an end'. Scott will not allow the argument that at least such casualness leads to greater lifelikeness and he offers an early rebuke to the fallacy of imitative form:

> It is true, that not only the practice of some great authors in this department, but even the general course of human life itself, may be quoted in favour of this more obvious, and less artificial practice, of arranging a narrative. It is seldom that the same circle of personages who have surrounded an individual at his first outset in life, continue to have an interest in his career till his fate comes to a crisis . . . But though such an unconnected course of adventures is what most frequently occurs in nature, yet the province of the romance writer being artificial, there is more required from him than a mere compliance with the simplicity of reality, — just as we demand from the scientific

gardener, that he shall arrange, in curious knots and artificial parterres, the flowers which 'nature boon' distributes freely on hill and dale.[12]

Fielding's superiority lies not simply in the mechanical skill of the plot – 'a story regularly built and consistent in all its parts' – but because scarcely a character is introduced who does not do something to advance the story: the plot and the characters are inseparable. But for all the high praise – Fielding is for Scott the greatest of all the novelists – he is not someone who can or, perhaps, should be imitated. The critic should not demand of other novelists Fielding's remarkable skill in plot production, for this would be 'to fetter too much the power of giving pleasure, by surrounding it with penal rules; since of this sort of light literature it may be especially said – *tout genre est permis, hors le genre ennuyeux*'. Even the construction and arrangement of the story in *Tom Jones* are inferior to the 'truth, force and spirit' of the characters. In his essay on Charlotte Smith, Scott, obviously thinking of his own practice and irritated by some early criticism of his own novels, writes with characteristic unease about plot:

> In time, whatever may be the vote of the severer critics, we are afraid that many of the labourers in this walk of literature will conclude with Bayes, by asking, 'what is the use of the plot but to bring in fine things?' And, truly, if the fine things really deserve the name, we think there is pedantry in censuring the works where they occur, merely because productions of genius are not also adorned with a regularity of conception, carrying skilfully forward the conclusion of the story, which we may safely pronounce one of the rarest attainments of art.[13]

On this subject Scott even goes from defence to attack, and in a remarkable passage in the Introduction (written in 1830) to *The Abbot* he suggests that a great and original writer has to educate the taste by which he is enjoyed.

Once more his comments on other writers confidently and accurately describe himself:

> Looking more attentively at the patriarchs of literature, whose career was as long as it was brilliant, I thought I perceived that, in the busy and prolonged course of exertion there were no doubt occasional failures, but that still those who were favourites of their age triumphed over these miscarriages. By the new efforts which they made, their errors were obliterated; they became identified with the literature of their country; and after having long received law from the critics, came in some degree to impose it.

Scott notes that new novels are not judged on their merits, but by ideas about fiction which readers have already formed from earlier writers, and that over such extrinsic ideas of fiction the new and original novelist may 'hope to triumph by patience and exertion'.

Since, then, it is force of character which is the first requirement of the novelist, it follows that psychological accuracy or truth of human nature will be more important than historical accuracy or truth in drawing the external world. Every successful novelist, says Scott, must be a poet, even if he has never written a line of verse. He explains this by adding that imagination is indispensable to the novelist who must 'examine and embody human character and human passion'. Richardson's great achievement was that he threw aside the trappings of romance and appealed 'to the genuine passions of the human heart'. Richardson's inaccuracies and anachronisms do not matter; he is a great writer because of the accuracy and truth with which he draws 'the light and shade of human passion' and because of his sympathetic imagination, his ability 'to throw himself into the character of his heroine, and to think and reason, and express those thoughts and reasons, exactly as she must have done had the fictitious

incident really befallen such a person'. But Scott quarrels
(for once) with Dr Johnson, who found that there was
'more knowledge of the human heart in one letter of
Richardson's than in all *Tom Jones*'. Scott, in his disagree-
ment, is more Augustan than Dr Johnson. Richardson is
prolix; he risks boring; too much of his detail is minute,
trivial and even uninteresting; he is too particular; he
'numbers the streaks of the tulip'. Fielding's truth to
nature is perhaps greater; *Tom Jones* is superior to every
earlier novel because it is 'truth and human nature itself'.

IV

In his criticism of novelists Scott returns many times to
the problem of the supernatural and how it should be
handled in fiction. The management of the supernatural
is 'a task of a most delicate nature'. He knew that he had
failed disastrously in *The Monastery* and was intrigued by
his own failure. With this exception (and perhaps because
of this exception) Scott's handling of the subject is expert
and assured; and supremely in 'Wandering Willie's Tale'
he reaches what Mary Lascelles calls 'the equilibrium between natural and supernatural'.[14] Scott's discussion of this
'delicate task' is not only intelligent, it helps us to see how
he gained his own successes when so many others failed.

The novels which lead him to discuss the supernatural
are *Frankenstein*, *The Castle of Otranto* and *The Mysteries
of Udolpho*. In general he considers Mary Shelley and
Horace Walpole to be successes and Mrs Radcliffe a
failure. Scott, indeed, did not like to be compared to Mrs
Radcliffe and complains in his Journal that 'James Ballan-
tyre is severely critical of what he calls imitations of Mrs
Radcliffe in *Woodstock* . . . I have taken a wide difference:
my object is not to excite fear of supernatural things in

my reader, but to show the effect of such fear upon the agents in the story'.[15] The emphasis is typical and fits in with his admiring comments on Mackenzie.

In 1818 in a review of *Frankenstein* in *Blackwood's Edinburgh Magazine* Scott wrote: 'The first general division of works of fiction, into such as bound the events they narrate by the actual laws of nature, and such as, passing these limits, are managed by marvellous and supernatural machinery is sufficiently obvious and decided. But the class of marvellous romances admits of several subdivisions.'[16] Scott's own practice is (typically) a compromise between these two, but he goes on to define further and to make important distinctions. In former times a writer who introduced the supernatural did not go against the laws of credibility since he and his readers firmly believed in the existence and the power of 'witches, goblins and magicians'. This faith is passing away. 'The popular belief no longer allows the possibility of existence to the race of mysterious beings which hovered betwixt this world and that which is invisible.' This does not settle the problem for a modern writer who deals with a former age in which such beliefs were held. Scott's example is *The Castle of Otranto*, which, he says, 'details supernatural incidents as they would have been readily believed in the eleventh or twelfth century'; and it is ambitious and valuable since Walpole hoped 'to wind up the feelings of his reader till they became for a moment identified with those of a ruder age'. Walpole's supernatural happenings were 'consistent with the belief of all mankind at [the period] in which the action is placed'. In a modern novel that deals with the past the supernatural is an allowable explanation of events; 'it is no great demand upon the reader's credulity to ask him to credit, as he reads about his ancestors, what they devoutly believed in'. But Scott, in his own practice, changed his mind; his experience in *The Monastery* convinced him that, even in a novel dealing with past ages, this was one suspension of disbelief that a modern reader could not be expected to make. In modern fiction the use of the supernatural is an indulgence. The supernatural is not simply the inexplicable cause of events, but becomes the principal object of the story and is described for its own sake. The supernatural and the marvellous become machinery, 'the resort of distressed authors since the days of Horace'; the machinery takes over, and the one great interest which the supernatural in fiction can offer, 'its effect upon the mind of the human personages engaged in its wonders', is scarcely treated. It is, indeed, possible to harness the impossible and the marvellous to the true humane purposes of fiction and to write a story 'in which the laws of nature are represented as altered, not for the purpose of pampering the imagination with wonders, but in order to show the probable effect which the supposed miracles would produce on those who witnessed them. In this case the pleasure ordinarily derived from the marvellous incident is secondary to that which we extract from observing how mortals like ourselves would be affected.' Scott is drawing a distinction between 'the marvellous and the effects of the marvellous' and contrasts the story of Tom Thumb with Gulliver's voyage to Brobdingnag. In the former case we are offered nothing but 'every species of hyperbole'. Gulliver, however fantastic the circumstances in which he is placed, always behaves 'according to the laws of probability and the nature of the human heart'.

Mary Shelley's *Frankenstein* is equally successful:

> although the formation of a thinking and sentient being by scientific skill is an incident of the fantastic character, still the interest of the work does not turn upon the marvellous creation

of Frankenstein's monster but upon the feelings and sentiments which that creature is supposed to express as most natural – if we may use the phrase – to his unnatural condition and origin. In other words the miracle is not wrought for the mere wonder, but is designed to give rise to a train of acting and reasoning in itself just and probable, although the *postulatum* on which it is grounded is in the highest degree extravagant.[17]

The impossible is not the improbable: 'we grant the extraordinary postulates which the author demands as the foundation of the narrative only on condition of his deducing the consequences with logical precision'. The appeal must always be made to nature; the worst incredibilities are those in the moral, not the physical world.

The compromise of Mrs Radcliffe and her successors is unsatisfactory. The marvellous and the supernatural abound in her novels, but she ends by 'referring her prodigies to an explanation founded on natural causes, in the latter chapters of her romances'. There are many objections to this. In place of the impossible we are offered the improbable; the explanation of the mystery is sometimes more unlikely than if it had been accounted for by a supernatural being. How can we take seriously 'the operation of fulminating powder, combined mirrors, magic lanterns, trap-doors, speaking-trumpets and suchlike apparatus of German phantasmagoria'? (In *The Antiquary* it is only the foolish Sir Arthur Wardour who takes these things seriously.) Such a method does not allow for the willing suspension of disbelief. A reader who is asked to accept that there is such a thing as supernatural agency 'throws his mind into the attitude best adopted to humour the deceit which is presented for his entertainment, and grants, for the time of perusal, the premises on which the fable depends'. Mrs Radcliffe's method is misguided; it deprives a second reading of any possible interest, and it

makes the whole interest of the novel depend on arousing
not so much our horror as our curiosity. It involves, too,
a difficult technical problem — how to overcome 'the
torment of romance-writers, those necessary evils, the con-
cluding chapters, when they must . . . account for all the
incidents which they have been at such pains to render
unaccountable.'

> Such are the difficulties and dilemmas which attend the path of
> the professed story-teller, who, while it is expected of him that
> his narrative should be interesting and extraordinary, is neither
> permitted to explain its wonders, by referring them to ordinary
> causes, on account of their triteness, nor to supernatural agency,
> because of its incredibility. It is no wonder that, hemmed in by
> rules so strict, Mrs Radcliffe, a mistress of the art of exciting
> curiosity, has not been uniformly fortunate in the mode of
> gratifying it.[18]

And the accounts are usually poor ones; it would be better
if, as with Walpole or Shakespeare, we were asked to
credit the possibility of the supernatural events and to
seek no explanation of them.

> We can believe, for example, in Macbeth's witches, and tremble
> at their spells; but had we been informed, in the conclusion of
> the piece, that they were only three of his wife's chamber-maids
> disguised for the purpose of imposing on the Thane's credulity,
> it would have added little to the credibility of the story, and
> entirely deprived it of interest.[19]

Scott's own attitude to the possibility of supernatural
appearances is one of cautious scepticism. What he implies in his comments on the witches in *Macbeth* can be
seen in some remarks in his *Demonology*. There he gives
as a 'very common instance' the apprehension which a
murderer has that the ghost of his victim stands at his
bedside. But belief in the supernatural is not necessary to

explain such appearances; 'In all or any of these cases who shall doubt that imagination, favoured by circumstances, has power to summon up to the organ of sight, spectres which only exist in the minds of those by whom their apparition seems to be witnessed.' The writer should not require the reader to believe in the supernatural, but he should not explain it by natural causes. Scott's solution and his practice are a middle way, and he sees it to have been Shakespeare's way in *Macbeth*:

> There are some modern authors, indeed who have endeavoured, ingeniously enough, to compound betwixt ancient faith and modern incredulity. They have exhibited phantoms, and narrated prophecies strangely accomplished without giving a defined or absolute opinion, whether these are to be referred to supernatural agency, or whether the apparitions were produced (no uncommon case) by an overheated imagination, and the presages apparently verified by a casual, though singular coincidence of circumstances . . . Perhaps, upon the whole, this is the most artful mode of terminating such a wonder, as it forms the means of compounding with the taste of two different classes of readers; those who, like children, demand that each particular circumstance and incident of the narrative shall be fully accounted for; and the more imaginative class, who resembling men that walk for pleasure through a moonlight landscape, are more teazed than edified by the intrusive minuteness with which some well-meaning companion disturbs their reveries, divesting stock and stone of the shadowy semblances in which fancy had dressed them, and pertinaciously restoring to them the ordinary forms and commonplace meanness of reality.[20]

This is, of course, Scott's method in *The Bride of Lammermoor* and in 'Wandering Willie's Tale', where he introduces the supernatural 'without giving a defined or absolute opinion'.

Scott's objection to the attempt to arouse fear, melancholy and horror for their own sakes in tales of the super-

natural appears most clearly in a comparison he makes of
a poem by Mrs Radcliffe, 'Address to Melancholy', to
Fletcher's 'Hence, all you vain delights'. Mrs Radcliffe's
poem focuses, for Scott, the crippling weakness of her
novels. Scott says simply of Fletcher's poem that 'the
human feeling is predominant', and the items in the
landscape 'are only secondary parts of the picture'. In
the 'Address to Melancholy' it is different:

> The accessories and accompaniments of melancholy are well-
> described, but they call for so much of our attention, that the
> feeling itself scarce solicits due regard. We are placed among
> melancholy objects, but our sadness is reflected from the scene,
> it is not the growth of our own minds . . . Something like this
> may be observed in Mrs Radcliffe's romances, where our curio-
> sity is too much interested about the evolution of the story to
> permit our feelings to be acted upon by the distresses of the hero
> and heroine.[21]

Her interest in the supernatural and then her foolish
explanations of what had seemed so mysterious and terri-
fying mean for Scott that she has nothing to offer to any
intelligent reader. He dismisses her with two indictments
which give us a glimpse of his own interests and achievement: 'Mrs Radcliffe rather walks in fairy-land than in
the region of realities, and . . . she has neither displayed
the command of the human passions, nor the insight
into the human heart, nor the observation of life and
manners which recommend other authors in the same
line.'[22] These things are Scott's strength.

It is not surprising that it was to Maria Edgeworth, a
novelist who had the qualities which Mrs Radcliffe
lacked, that Scott confessed himself most indebted. Scott
never wearied in his praise of Maria Edgeworth or in his
acknowledgement of this debt. The story of their friend-
ship and mutual respect and admiration is entertaining

and attractive, and her visit to Scott at Edinburgh and Abbotsford was a high point in Scott's life. Lockhart records that her stay at Abbotsford made the month of August 1823 'one of the happiest in Scott's life. Never did I see a brighter day at Abbotsford than that on which Miss Edgeworth first arrived there – never can I forget her look and accent when she was received by him at his archway, and exclaimed, "Everything about you is exactly what one ought to have had wit to dream!"'[23]

Scott tells in the General Preface to his novels how about 1805 he had begun a novel called *Waverley* and had gone as far as the seventh chapter. The manuscript was then laid aside and entirely forgotten. One of the circumstances that recalled it to mind and gave him the wish to complete it was 'the triumphs of Miss Edgeworth which worked in me emulation and disturbed my indolence'. And in 'A Postscript which should have been a Preface' to *Waverley* he again records that in that novel it was his wish to describe the persons in his novel 'not by a caricatured and exaggerated use of the national dialect, but by their habits, manners and feelings; so as in some degree to emulate the admirable Irish portraits drawn by Miss Edgeworth'. Scott repeatedly tells us what he admired in her work. There is 'her remarkable power for embodying national character'; there is 'the exquisite truth and power of her characters'; there is her 'wonderful powers of vivifying all her persons, and making them live as real beings in your mind'. And she has 'a merit transcendant in my eyes, of raising your national character in the scale of public estimation, and making the rest of the British Empire acquainted with the peculiar and interesting character of a people too long neglected and too severely oppressed'. Scott felt that in writing *Waverley* he was close to Maria Edgeworth, since he wished the success of the book 'to depend upon the characters much more than upon the story'.

But none of this does anything to disturb the huge originality of Scott. He may have thought that in *Waverley* (and especially in the first seven chapters) he was offering, like Maria Edgeworth, a description of 'habits, manners and feelings'; and, as Professor Hart points out, Scott later gave us a '"manners" panorama of the *Nigel-Kenilworth-Peveril* kind'.[24] But it is not in these novels that we look for Scott's originality. Maria Edgeworth inspired Scott to write, but she did not influence him. He wished to be influenced by her and intended to be influenced by her, but what he wrote was something quite different.

Castle Rackrent (1800) is Maria Edgeworth's finest work, but it is not an historical novel. George Watson calls it

the first regional novel in English, and perhaps in all Europe; and as Scott saw at once, the regional novel is the gateway to the ampler world of the historical novel since it represents whole societies and conceives of individual characters as composing societies . . . *Rackrent* pictures a world identified in time and place . . .[25]

But for Maria Edgeworth the time is past and the place is dead. '*Rackrent* is a novel of optimism: it is about a bad old day that is dead and gone';[26] and Maria Edgeworth makes the same point in her Preface to the novel:

The Editor hopes his readers will observe that these are 'tales of other times'; that the manners depicted in the following pages are not those of the present age: the race of the Rackrents has long since been extinct in Ireland, and the drunken Sir Patrick, the litigious Sir Murtagh, the fighting Sir Kit, and the slovenly Sir Condy, are characters which could no more be met with at present in Ireland, than Squire Western or Parson Trulliber in England.[27]

Maria Edgeworth is a social novelist. She can recreate a past society in *Castle Rackrent*, or (less interestingly) can describe in *The Absentee* (1812) the social changes that followed the Union. She is a regional novelist if by this is meant a novel in which the characters 'evolve from their natural vicinage . . . are living representations who speak in the diction of their locale and who move about in cognizance of the habits and customs of the place';[28] but she is not a historical novelist. George Watson makes a distinction: 'The novel [*Rackrent*] is historical as well as regional, in fact – and if we hesitate to call it an "historical novel" it is only because, unlike *Waverley*, it celebrates no great public event like the Forty-Five.'[29] But if *Castle Rackrent* is not a historical novel this is not because it 'celebrates' no great event like the '45. Many of Scott's novels – *Redgauntlet, The Fair Maid of Perth, St Ronan's Well* – deal with no great public event and are yet profoundly historical; and in no sense does *Waverley* 'celebrate' the '45. *Castle Rackrent* is not a historical novel because, unlike Scott's great fictions, it shows the past as dead, with no power to erupt into the present. It gives no sense of any dynamic movement in history which leads to the present and will lead beyond it. In Maria Edgeworth's novels the emphasis is on the past as 'the end of an auld sang'; in Scott 'theme is never focused on what is *done* but on what is still alive, still redeemable, still unresolved',[30] and on the constant crisis for the individual as, through intelligence, courage and imagination, he learns to adapt and survive.

Because, for Maria Edgeworth, the past is irredeemable and dead, her interest in observed Irish characteristics is 'restricted to their *peculiarity* and she had little sympathy with or curiosity about the underlying modes of thought or views of life which made them individual'.[31]

This limitation, this interest in 'peculiarity', comes out even in her excellent renderings of peasant speech, where the dialect or idiomatic phrases are reproduced for their quaintness, and are printed in italics. Scott's originality lies in his profound examination of the meaning of history.

2 Scott and History

He understood what History meant. (CARLYLE)

CARLYLE'S comment on learning of Scott's death is generous but vague. What, we soon ask, *did* history mean to Scott. If we turn to his essay on Scott for further explanation we find, disappointingly, that Carlyle does not mean very much by his epigraph.

> these Historical Novels have taught all men this truth, which looks like a truism, and yet was as good as unknown to writers of history and others, till so taught: that the bygone ages of the world were actually filled by living men, not by protocols, state-papers, controversies and abstractions of men. Not abstractions were they, not diagrams and theorems; but men, in buff or other coats and breeches, with colour in their cheeks, with passions in their stomach, and the idioms, features and vitalities of very men. It is a little word; inclusive of great meaning! [1]

This is, of course, an important part of Scott's achievement; for Victorian critics it was perhaps the most important thing to say about Scott and History, and to contemporary readers it must have been the most radical and exciting element in the Waverley novels. Today this would not be enough to establish Scott's importance, though his ability to make the past vivid still has large appeal. Carlyle's delight is echoed by Professor G. M. Young, who talks of

> the revolution effected by Scott in the writing of history, and particularly of mediaeval history. The secret is to treat every document as the record of a conversation, and go on reading till

you hear the people speaking. And that is, or will be, the key-
word of the new school. 'What happened here?' the older
generation might ask. 'No battle was fought, no treaty was
signed, no council assembled – pass on.' Their successors will
answer, 'People were talking. Let us stop and listen.' [2]

Scott's ability to listen, it seems, is his chief historical
merit. Professor Young does not suggest that Scott either
comments on events or considers the question 'Why did
it happen?' In the same essay he categorises further and
by implication sets a lower value on Scott. He distinguishes two sorts of historical theme, the logical and the
psychological: 'One, having set its zero hour, undertakes
to show how and why things happened as they did, and
the other what did it feel like to be alive when they were
happening'.[3] Professor Young is naturally aware that
there is more to Scott's attitude towards history than this.
He says, very briefly and tantalisingly, that Scott knew the
object of history to be 'nothing less than the setting forth
of an entire culture'. He does not expand the remark
(except to say that the twelfth chapter of *The Bride of
Lammermoor* describes the breakdown of feudal economy
at Wolf's-hope), but it suggests that Scott's intentions or
achievements are not so simple as is still sometimes
thought.

'Intentions' is perhaps the wrong word to use about so
untheoretic a writer as Scott. He seldom commented on
the aims or intentions of his novels, or on what he felt an
historical novel should do. We have not much more than
a few sentences in the Dedicatory Epistle to *Ivanhoe* and
a metaphor in the opening chapter of *Waverley*. Scott's
modesty is notorious, and misleading; one of the points
he insists on in the Dedicatory Epistle is that he does not
aim at total and detailed historical accuracy, and is not at
all sure that an historical novel should.

It is true that I neither can nor do pretend to the observation of complete accuracy, even in matters of outward costume, much less in the more important points of language and manners. But the same motive which prevents my writing the dialogue of the piece in Anglo-Saxon or in Norman-French, and which prohibits my sending forth to the public this essay printed with the types of Caxton or Wynken de Worde, prevents my attempting to confine myself within the limits of the period in which my story is laid. It is necessary, for exciting interest of any kind, that the subject assumed should be, as it were translated into the manners, as well as the language, of the age we live in.

Scott took liberties in matters of detail. In *The Abbot* Queen Mary watches the defeat of her army from Crookstone Castle. Scott was later informed that he had mistaken Crookstone Castle for Cathcart Castle. He made no change in subsequent editions of the novel, but acknowledged the correction in a note: 'I was led astray in the present case . . . by a traditionary report of Mary having seen the battle from the Castle of Crookstone, which seemed so much to increase the interest of the scene that I have been unwilling to make, in this particular instance, the fiction give way to the fact . . .' The reason may not have been serious, and, in fact, Scott was generally strong in details of this kind; but he knew they did not matter, and he was right to insist that it was neither his task nor the task of any historical novelist to achieve accuracy of this kind. Sir Herbert Grierson brings Aristotle to Scott's support, and reminds us that 'the concern of the poet is not with what actually did happen, but with what might happen now or might have happened at such or such a definite period of history, so far as we have acquired a sufficient knowledge and understanding of the period in question'.[4] A slavish accuracy in historical detail will be false to the spirit and truth of history and implies a single and narrow view of what history means.

If the historical novelist regards his duty as being to avoid anachronisms, history will seem to him a chain. The different condition of things existing in the period of which he writes will be a source of labour to him, and a pitfall. But to the true historical novelist they are a glory, they are the whole point of his work, and what was a weakness becomes a strength. If a writer wishes to 'work up' a period in order to set a story in it, he will feel history a fetter and every unexpected fact may hamper the story he intended to tell. But if he has steeped his mind in some past age, and has lived in that age, turning it over and over in his imagination, realising the conditions of affairs and the relationships of men and pondering over the implications of these and so recasting the life of the age for himself, then that particular age and those special conditions will suggest their own story, and the historical peculiarities of that age will give point to his novel and will become a power. There is all the difference in the world between a man who has a story to tell and wishes to set it in a past age and to adjust it to the demands of history, and the man who has the past in his head and allows it to come forth in story.[5]

We should not expect the historical novelist to retell the story of great events. 'What matters is that we should re-experience the social and human motives which led men to think, feel and act as they did in historical reality.'[6] The historical novel need have no 'real' historical person; no incident in it need ever 'really' have happened. 'The novelist who seeks to tell things that "really happened" must clutch at episodes.'[7] Only the world in which the characters are placed, 'the currents that sweep over their lives, and the movements that overwhelm them need to be real'.[8] The historical novel may be 'true to history without being true to fact'. A more modern way of expressing it is to say that Scott makes 'imaginative models of real historical processes and their inner conflicts'.[9]

These points are well dramatised in *Redgauntlet*. The

main action and the main character in the story (set in
1763 or 1764) are wholly fictional. The Young Pretender
never returned to Scotland to make one final attempt for
the Crown, and no such person as Redgauntlet ever
existed. Scott uses this fiction, this picture of a Jacobite
'who still cherished a lingering though hopeless attachment to the House of Stewart' to interpret to us the nature
and inevitable decline of Jacobitism, and to say something
about the inevitability and necessity of all historical change.
He dramatises the social circumstances that have brought
about this change, and personifies in Joshua Geddes, the
Quaker, that 'gradual influx of wealth and extension of
commerce' which Scott sees as chiefly responsible. *Redgauntlet*, through characters like Alan Fairford, Geddes,
Provost Crosbie, Redgauntlet himself, Alan's father and
others, gives us the chance 'to re-experience the social and
human motives which led men to think, feel and act just
as they did in historical reality'. But it does more; to go
back to Grierson, it shows us what might have happened
in history; it offers us the true shape of history; it is not
truth of fact but 'an imaginative model of a real historical
process and its inner conflict'. And it is one thing more:
a moving comment on the need for change and the price
to be paid for it.

But to talk of 'the true shape of history' and of 'historical process' is to jump ahead. In the Dedicatory Epistle
to *Ivanhoe* and in the first chapter of *Waverley* Scott
touches on something more important than historical
accuracy but connected to it. Is human nature a constant?
Have the human passions been the same at all times and
in all countries? If it is a constant, then too fussy a con-
centration on ephemeral detail will detract from that
general truth which it is the novelist's task to provide. It
is, as Donald Davie says, 'one of the most serious ques-

tions that can be asked of the whole "Waverley" series, whether in these novels Scott believes in a constant "nature" in this sense, or not'.[10] If you believe that human nature is unalterable; that 'amidst all the disorder and inequality which variety of discipline, example, conversation, and employment, produce in the intellectual advances of different men, there is still discovered . . . such a general . . . similitude as may be expected in the same common nature affected by external circumstances indefinitely varied',[11] then you will not see history as process. What such a question raises is the nature of Scott's historicism.

It is, of course, unwise, to rely on Scott's explicit references: only the novels themselves can make plain what Scott thought history meant. But his few explicit comments are valuable because they show he is aware of the question, and because they make clear, through all the uncertainty with which he discusses it, that there will be no simple answer to it in his novels. In the first chapter of *Waverley* he writes:

> By fixing, then, the date of my story Sixty Years before the present 1st November 1805, I would have my readers understand that they will meet in the following pages neither a romance of chivalry nor a tale of modern manners . . . From this my choice of an era, the understanding critic may further presage that the object of my tale is more a description of men than manners.

(It is interesting that Scott, in echoing Fielding's phrase — 'I describe not men, but manners; not an individual, but a species' — should invert it and yet mean what Fielding means. A page later Scott explains that he writes 'from the great book of Nature, the same through a thousand editions'.)

Considering the disadvantages inseparable from this part of my subject, I must be understood to have resolved to avoid them as much as possible, by throwing the force of my narrative upon the characters and passions of the actors – those passions common to men in all stages of society, and which have alike agitated the human heart, whether it throbbed under the steel corselet of the fifteenth century, the brocaded coat of the eighteenth, or the blue frock and white dimity waistcoat of the present day. Upon these passions it is no doubt true that the state of manners and laws casts a necessary colouring; but the bearings, to use the language of heraldry, remain the same, though the tincture may be not only different, but opposed in strong contradistinction.

Donald Davie is right to remind us that if this 'constitutes a plea for the thoroughly neo-classical principle that the business of the artist is with "nature", meaning by that the constant elements in human nature to be detected beneath the adventitious distinctions of period, race and trade',[12] the sentences come from one of the chapters written in 1805 and do not aptly describe the rest of the novel written about seven years later. From the reluctant, 'Upon these passions it is no doubt true that the state of manners and laws casts a necessary colouring', and from the dismissive 'tincture', Scott later came to give 'bearings' and 'tincture' more equal weight.

For many readers of Scott today Scott's understanding of history was possible only when he began to qualify (the Marxists would say that he shed it) the Enlightenment view that human nature was unchangeable. The qualification is clearer by the time of the Dedicatory Epistle to *Ivanhoe*:

In point of justice, therefore, to the multitudes who will, I trust, devour this book with avidity, I have so far explained our ancient manners in modern language, and so far detailed the characters and sentiments of my persons, that the modern reader will not find himself, I should hope, much trammelled by the repulsive dryness of mere antiquity. In this, I respectfully contend, I have in no respect exceeded the fair license due to the author of a fictitious composition. The late ingenious Mr Strutt, in his romance of Queen-Hoo-Hall, acted upon another principle; and in distinguishing between what was ancient and modern, forgot, as it appears to me, that extensive neutral ground, the large proportion, that is of manners and sentiments which are common to us and to our ancestors, having been handed down unaltered from them to us, or which, arising out of the principles of our common nature, must have existed alike in either state of society . . . What I have applied to language, is still more justly applicable to sentiments and manners. The passions, the sources from which these must spring in all their modifications, are generally the same in all ranks and conditions, all countries and ages; and it follows, as a matter of course, that the opinions, habits of thinking, and actions, however influenced by the peculiar state of society, must still, upon the whole, bear a strong resemblance to each other. Our ancestors were not more distinct from us, surely, than Jews are from Christians; they had 'eyes, hands, organs, dimensions, senses, affections, passions;' were 'fed with the same food, hurt with the same weapons, subject to the same diseases, warmed and cooled by the same winter and summer,' as ourselves. The tenor, therefore, of their affections and feelings must have borne the same general proportion to our own.

Alexander Welsh says of the closing sentences that 'Scott hesitates . . . as if he were aware of the impending surge of historicism.'[13] It is certainly not the language of someone totally convinced that human nature is the one fixed point in history. As we should expect from a novelist whose characteristic method is to offer the clash of opposing forces, and who through his mediocre heroes and comic characters offers us a middle way, Scott's historicism is not simple; it is a compromise and cannot be easily defined. Scott sees the past as inevitably leading to the present, but sees that the present itself is no resting place. The present is not necessarily superior to the past; its importance is simply that it *is* the present. He does not exploit the remoteness of the past but shows its closeness to the present. The nostalgia that Scott might feel for the earlier culture represented by Redgauntlet, or Vich Ian Vohr, or Rob Roy is checked by his recognition that history is movement, change, very often progress and necessarily leads to the present. There is no condescension towards the past; what was of value there was valuable indeed, but it is not permanent, it is simply part of a process (battles, as we saw, are irrelevant) which leads to a probably more valuable present. (Scott never tired of praising Sir Humphry Davy and his safety-lamp.) His interest is in the dynamic movement of history. 'His best novels', Leslie Stephen said, 'might all be described as "Tales of My Grandfather".'[14] They catch and dramatise history at a moment of critical change. Scott deals with great crises in history and sees much of his own advantage as a historical novelist to lie in the fact that he is living in such a time of crisis himself. He writes his novels about turning-points in history; he is not narrowly the historian of Jacobitism, or even of Scotland, but the historian of every historical crisis or crux and of men's reactions to such crises. In the Introduction to *Quentin Durward* Scott writes: 'The scene of this romance is laid in the fifteenth century, when the feudal system . . . and the spirit of chivalry began to be innovated upon and abandoned.' And all the Scottish novels dramatise historical crisis, a sudden great leap forward; but it is the crisis as much as the Scottishness that interests Scott and makes him far more than the novelist of manners he aimed to be. In the Introduction to the *Chronicles of the Canongate* Scott (under the name of Mr Croftangry) says to an elderly woman:

The Highlands . . . should furnish you with ample subjects of recollection. You have witnessed the complete change of that primeval country, and have seen a race not far removed from the earliest period of society melted down into the great mass of civilization; and that could not happen without incidents striking in themselves, and curious as chapters in the history of the human race.

What happens in Scotland is something inevitable in all history. If it is true that Scott's best novels are generally about Scotland, and often about the Scotland of the fairly recent past, this is simply because his nearness to such crisis enables him to dramatise it in Scottish types and characters and their living language.

Because he sees history in terms of crisis, the difficult movement forward from a more primitive to a newer way of life, it is often a dramatic contrast which tempts him to write. He acknowledges in the General Preface to the Waverley novels that it was this awareness of contrast that tempted him to write: 'It naturally occurred to me that the ancient traditions and high spirit of a people who, living in a civilised age and country, retained so strong a tincture of manners belonging to an early period of society, must afford a subject favourable for romance . . .' In the Introduction to *The Monastery* Scott writes:

The general plan of the story was, to conjoin two characters . . . who, thrown into situations which gave them different views on the subject of the Reformation, should . . . dedicate themselves, the one to the support of the sinking fabric of the Catholic Church, the other to the establishment of the Reformed doctrines.

It is this interest that stops any nostalgic note from damaging those novels that deal with eighteenth-century Scotland. If *Waverley* and *Redgauntlet* imply that with the destruction of the clan system something elusive but fine in manners and conduct and spirit has been lost, Scott does not suggest that such a decline can be dated from any one time – after the '45 or after the Reformation. He merely uses any historical moment when men felt that a glory had passed (or was passing) away (the early years of King James I's reign in *The Fortunes of Nigel*, the reign of Robert III in *The Fair Maid of Perth*) to focus attention on the nature of inevitable historical change, the price, in human terms, that has to be paid for it, and the need always to adapt and survive such change with skill and honour. He can make the recent past real more easily than the Middle Ages, not because he can supply with accuracy a greater wealth of concrete detail, but because he can show that past to be the necessary 'pre-history of the present'. His knowledge of the recent past was greater than his knowledge of any other. He knew about the recent past in Scotland – its society and politics and economy, the way the people lived and how they felt. His knowledge is not given in a static or analytic way, but comes to us through 'his capacity to give living human embodiment to historical-social types. The typically human terms in which great historical trends become tangible had never before been so superbly, straight-forwardly and pregnantly portrayed.'[15] But Scott cannot be taken over by the Marxists, though his understanding of the relationship between the individual and society is such that a Marxist interpretation of Scott's historicism can carry conviction. Arnold Kettle rightly says of Jeanie Deans's refusal to perjure herself to save her sister's life that 'History is behind it, the history of generations of lowland peasants fighting for the right'.[16]

Georg Lukács writes:

With the suppression of the uprising of 1745 – which is depicted In Waverley – the real downfall of gentile society in Scotland begins, says Engels. Several decades later [*sic*] (in *Rob Roy*) we see the clans already in a state of complex economic dissolution. One character in this novel, the shrewd merchant and bailiff of Glasgow, Jarvie, clearly sees that it has become a matter of economic necessity for the clans to wage their desperate and hopeless battle on behalf of the Stuarts. They are no longer able to maintain themselves on the basic of their primitive economy. They possess a surplus population, permanently armed and well seasoned who cannot be put to any normal use, who must resort to plunder and pillage, and for whom an uprising of this kind is the only way out of a hopeless situation. Thus we have here already an element of dissolution, the beginnings of class-uprooting which were as yet absent from the clan picture of *Waverley*.

Once more we must admire here Scott's extraordinarily realistic presentation of history, his ability to translate these new elements of economic and social change into human fates, into an altered psychology.[17]

The mistake in putting *Rob Roy* at a later date than *Waverley* is interesting. It is because the clans are in a state of economic dissolution that the events of *Waverley* (the 1745 rebellion) and their result are inevitable. But if we can agree with much of what Lukács says, he is false to Scott and the effect of the novels when he relates 'economic and social change' so closely to an 'altered psychology'. Scott's understanding of history is greater — great enough to make so firm a logic impossible.

Marx, like Hegel, insisted that human history is not a number of different parallel histories, economic, political, artistic, religious, and so on, but one single history. But like Hegel, again, he conceived this unity not as an organic unity in which every thread of the developing process preserved its own continuity as well as its intimate connexion with the others, but as a unity in which there was only one continuous thread (in Hegel the thread of political history, in Marx that of economic history) . . .[18]

Scott offers a different continuous thread. 'Without some assumption of basic uniformity [in human nature] neither history nor art is possible.'[19] This notion of a basic uniformity is what delights and instructs us in Scott's portrayal of characters. Bailie Nicol Jarvie is, in Lukács's phrase, a 'living human embodiment of an historical-social type'. He represents the new and growing commercial Scotland; he is the man of the future, a successful man whose success consists in moving from past to present. He is distantly related to Rob Roy; his insistence on this relationship emphasises the difference and distance between them, and suggests how anachronistic is the way of life represented by Rob Roy. (Rob Roy himself sees there is no future for his children in such a way of life; and if he spurns Jarvie's well-meant offer to find them jobs in the Glasgow mills, that, after all, is where many sons of Rob Roy have since gone.) The most famous scene in this novel is the fight at the clachan of Aberfoil; and the scene is memorable (though short) because of its symbolic force. Jarvie's sword is 'rusty' (the future does not lie with the sword). He forces his opponent to retreat (with a firebrand) and so acts out the defeat of an older, heroic past by a commercial and less glamorous present. The Bailie is for Credit as opposed to Honour – that Honour represented by Rob Roy and towards which Frank Osbaldistone is nostalgically drawn.

All this is true, but it is not quite everything. The bailie is not simply the 'embodiment of an historical-social type'. He is a type of human being that is always with us – vain, loquacious, smug, kind-hearted – though the 'tincture' may be different in different ages. That Scott meant his characters to supply the continuous thread in history is shown by his fondness for giving them names after the manner of Fielding: Fairservice,

Mailsetter, Mucklewrath, even Rashleigh and Waverley.

Frank Osbaldistone's father (in *Rob Roy*) may represent the commercial values of eighteenth-century England. Scott's interpretation of him is indeed 'a genuine contribution to the understanding of history, to the drawing of a distinction between Capitalism in its first expansive and adventurous phase, and the capitalism of a later age that is above all prudent and cautious'.[20] But this does not wholly explain our delight in him, or in Bailie Nicol Jarvie, or in Alan Fairford's father in *Redgauntlet*. Our delight is similar in kind (but greater) to the delight which Fielding offers when he draws the lawyer in the stage-coach in *Joseph Andrews*.

> The lawyer is not only alive, but hath been so these four thousand years; and I hope G—— will indulge his life as many yet to come. He hath not indeed confined himself to one profession, one religion or one country; but when the first mean selfish creature appeared on the human stage, who made self the centre of the whole creation, would give himself no pain, incur no danger, advance no money, to assist or preserve his fellow-creatures; then was our lawyer born; and, whilst such a person as I have described exists on earth, so long shall he remain upon it.[21]

Scott does not try to explain character wholly in terms of social or economic or other conditions of the time. He follows a complex middle way between an Enlightenment view of history, with human nature as the one great and totally fixed point, and an historicist approach to the past. 'His recreated past was peopled not only by concrete individuals but by historical forces as well';[22] and his 'series of novels . . . illuminate a particular period and throws light on human character in general . . . it was his tendency to look at history through character and at character through the history that had worked on it that provided the foundation of his art'.[23]

Scott, then, is supremely the historian of the recent past. He portrays great crises in (especially) Scottish history and sees each crisis producing a compromise; the 'truth' of the history of England and Scotland is the middle way, the famous English compromise: this is, in part, what History meant to him.

> Thus, out of the struggle of the Saxons and Normans there arose the English nation, neither Saxon nor Norman; in the same way the bloody Wars of the Roses gave rise to the illustrious reign of the House of Tudor, especially that of Queen Elizabeth; and those class struggles which manifested themselves in the Cromwellian Revolution were finally evened out in the England of today, after a long period of uncertainty and civil war, by the 'Glorious Revolution' and its aftermath.[24]

But he enlarges the historical crisis to make it both a personal crisis and one of permanent general value. At a time of great change, when Scott could see the transformation from the Scotland of his grandfathers ('There is no European nation, which, within the course of half a century, or little more, has undergone so complete a change as this Kingdom of Scotland'),[25] he saw the crucial compromise not as that between Saxon and Norman, Jacobite and Hanoverian, but between Past and Present. He deals with the recent past because through it he can more easily dramatise the process of change and the need to survive such change.

> Theme is never focused on what is *done* but on what is still alive, still redeemable, still unresolved. Every past scene is in the present. The times in such pasts are always out of control; the question is always how to live with, how morally to survive such times, such presents, and how to stabilize the present by redeeming the past.[26]

Scott sees that the process of history forces on the individual the need for adaptation and change. There is no indulged nostalgia in the novels, but only a recognition of the need to move from past to present, and an awareness of the price that has to be paid.

The problem of such survival was a personal one for Scott, and a problem for society, for Scotland. The heroism of Vich Ian Vohr and Rob Roy and Redgauntlet is at last anachronistic; Scott's epic heroes are always defeated. They are either killed or, like Flora Mac-Ivor and Redgauntlet, retire from the world to convent or monastery. (Sir Hildebrand Osbaldistone and all his sons die; Frank inherits their estate.) But it was something larger – a problem of adjustment of general and permanent and increasing value. 'If the Author of Waverley's study in the politics of survival is not still timely, it is hard to know one that is.'[27]

Something of all this can be illustrated from *The Bride of Lammermoor* or from the short story 'The Highland Widow'. In *The Bride of Lammermoor* (to be discussed later) the failure to move from past to present is less evident in political or social terms; but we can see in it more clearly than elsewhere that Scott is not narrowly or only concerned with a great crisis in social or political history, but with a great personal and private crisis which is always with us, even if the 'tincture' of the crisis is determined by a political-economic or cultural situation.

Scott thought well of 'The Highland Widow', and said it was in his 'bettermost manner'. It is another tale of 'Sixty Years Since' and the action takes place shortly after the '45. Elspat MacTavish was the wife of Hamish MacTavish, the leader of a gang of Highland caterans. Hamish MacTavish's habits were 'of the old Highland stamp which esteemed it shame to want anything that could be had for the taking'; and the morality of Hamish and Elspat 'was of the old Highland cast – faithful friends and fierce enemies'.

Hamish had been active for the Prince in 1745; he had been outlawed as a traitor to the state and as a robber, and was eventually caught and killed by English soldiers. Elspat's one consolation was that she had a son who might be trained to behave and believe as his parents behaved and believed, and who might achieve the kind of fame which his father had. Like Redgauntlet, Elspat cannot see that times have changed, and will not see any need to change her ways of thinking and living: 'she was quite unconscious of the great change which had taken place in the country around her – the substitution of civil order for military violence, and the strength gained by the law and its adherents over those who were called in Gaelic song, "the stormy sons of the sword". Her son, however, as he grows up, is freer of the past, and sees that the courage and skill which he has inherited from his parents must be used in different ways:

> Much attached to his mother, and disposed to do all in his power for her support, Hamish yet perceived, when he mixed with the world, that the trade of the cateran was now alike dangerous and discreditable, and that if he were to emulate his father's prowess, it must be in some other line of warfare more consonant to the opinions of the present day.

For Elspat time stands still, and her son speaks to her eloquently but in vain:

> 'Dearest mother', answered Hamish, 'how shall I convince you that you live in this land of our fathers as if our fathers were yet living? You walk as it were in a dream, surrounded by the phantoms of those who have been long with the dead. When my father lived and fought, the great respected the man of the

strong right hand, and the rich feared him . . . That is ended, and his son would only earn a disgraceful and unpitied death by the practices which gave his father credit and power among those who wear the breacan. The land is conquered; its lights are quenched – Glengarry, Lochiel, Perth, Lord Lewis, all the high chiefs, are dead or in exile. We may mourn for it, but we cannot help it. Bonnet, broadsword, and sporran – power, strength, and wealth, were all lost on Drummossie Muir.

Elspat 'viewed the present state of society with the same feelings with which she regarded the times that had passed away'. Two such conflicting views cannot exist together, and Hamish, literally, leaves his mother's world (it has no future; he calls it a 'desert') and enlists in one of the new Scottish regiments being raised to fight against the French in America. When Elspat is told that her son has been executed for returning late to his regiment and sees that this happened through her own selfish folly, she cannot at first believe it. Her son's death focuses her attitude towards the past; she had tried to make her son in the image of the past, in the image of his father, and can no longer accept or recognise that as her son had said, 'Yesterday was yesterday and today is today.' Like so many other Scott characters she withdraws from a world that she cannot accept: 'From that day the world was to her a wilderness, in which she remained without thought, care, or interest, absorbed in her own grief, indifferent to everything else.' Scott dramatises this withdrawal still further. In Elspat's final illness she manages to leave her wretched cottage unnoticed by the two women who had come to attend her final moments:

They sought brake, rock, and thicket in vain. Two hours after daylight, the minister himself appeared, and, on the report of the watchers, caused the country to be alarmed, and a general and exact search to be made through the whole neighbourhood of the cottage and the oak-tree. But it was all in vain. Elspat Mac-Tavish was never found, whether dead or alive; nor could there ever be traced the slightest circumstance to indicate her fate.

The problem of survival for a community or a nation is dramatised in terms of a personal failure or success.

There is no hero in *The Bride of Lammermoor* or 'The Highland Widow'. Scott's heroes are those who can survive the change from past to present, who can move with the times and profit by them. (And 'profit' very often in a very literal way. Many of Scott's 'successful' men are successful in business or trade: Frank Osbaldistone's father and Bailie Nicol Jarvie in *Rob Roy*, Joshua Geddes in *Redgauntlet*, Neil Blane in *Old Mortality*. His 'unsuccessful' men are often impoverished: Ravenswood, Redgauntlet, Peter Peebles.) Scott's heroes are in the fullest sense 'historical' heroes, and most historical when most fictional. They are of different kinds. There are those 'wooden' heroes who have never been popular with readers. Professor Daiches has commented on their peripatetic nature:

> Many of Scott's novels take the form of a sort of pilgrim's progress: an Englishman or a Lowland Scot goes north into the Highlands of Scotland at a time when Scottish feeling is running high, becomes involved in the passions and activities of the Scots partly by accident and partly by sympathy, and eventually extricates himself – physically altogether but emotionally not quite wholly – and returns whence he came . . . It is not this character but what he becomes involved in that matters: his function is merely to observe, react and withdraw.[28]

The implied opposition here, or tension, which runs through all Scott's best novels was first pointed out by Coleridge.

> The essential wisdom and happiness of the subject consists in this, – that the contest between the loyalists and their opponents

can never be *osbolete*, for it is the contest between the two great
moving principles of social humanity; religious adherence to the
past and the ancient, the desire and the admiration of perma-
nence on the one hand; and the passion for increase of knowledge,
for truth, as the offspring of reason – in short, the mighty
instincts of *progression* and *free agency*, on the other.[29]

The 'wooden' hero is a passive hero, but he is not neutral;
'He stands committed to prudence and the superiority of
civil society . . . He is committed to the civil, and observes
the uncivil.'[30] He is finally not simply an observer but a
critic of what he sees. But his conclusions are not quite
Scott's. He is often mocked by Scott, not simply because
of the early romantic errors which lead him astray, but
because of the ease and speed with which he rejects his
romantic views, and because of his failure to see the
tragedy and loss that lie behind all such rejection.

But Scott sees them. After the rearguard action at
Clifton, Waverley is separated from the Highland army
and finds shelter for a time at the house of a young
farmer. In his enforced idleness Waverley has time to
reflect on what has happened to him:

> it was in many a walk by the shores of Ullswater, that he ac-
> quired a more complete mastery of a spirit tamed by adversity,
> than his former experience had given him; and that he felt him-
> self entitled to say firmly, though perhaps with a sigh, that the
> romance of his life was ended, and that its real history had now
> commenced.

This 'real history' is the 'real history' of the Waverley
novels; it is the story of survival from past to present. If
the words 'perhaps with a sigh' suggest no great depth of
feeling, no estimate of the price of such change on
Waverley's part, it is through the Baron Bradwardine
(in spite of his absurdity) that Scott conveys something of

his understanding of what the destruction of a heroic past means. The Baron, after the failure of the '45, recognises the inevitability of change, the facts of 'real history'. When Waverley returns to the ruined house of Tully-Veolan he hears a voice singing the 'Border Widow's Lament'. It is the daft gardener, Davie Gellatley. All he can say is 'A' dead and gane – a' dead and gane'.

Mention of Baron Bradwardine should remind us that these middle-of-the-road heroes are neither Scott's most frequent nor most effective examples of his admiration for those who survive. Professor Daiches claims that the essence of the novels is the way in which conflicting claims impinge on the titular hero.[31] But this is to say too little. It implies that the essential narrative shape of the novel centres on the hero, and ignores the fact that it is generally Scott's comic characters who are the true heroes, who gain Scott's fullest esteem and who carry the meaning of his novels. They recognise that personal and national survival depend on changing with the times, on moving successfully from past to present. In *Rob Roy* there is Bailie Nicol Jarvie. In *Redgauntlet* there is Provost Crosbie, a Justice of the Peace who sympathises with the Jacobites and is distantly related to Redgauntlet. He is a successful merchant; he does not wish the old times back, but he knows that with their passing, something rare and fine and heroic has passed too. In the same novel there is 'Wandering Willie's Tale', that great story which summarises so much of what Scott says in his novels about history and our reaction to it. Steenie Steenson survives great political changes with skill and safety and even honour. He behaves with courage to get a receipt and lives successfully through a revolution. Above all there is Dugald Dalgetty in *A Legend of Montrose*.

But for the great heroic figures in Scott the world is too

much. They make dramatic gestures and simple choices in a world where neither is possible. They do not know what history means, that it is movement and crisis, and that personal and national survival depend on directing the crisis and turning it to account.

3 'Waverley'

. . . and there's the end of an auld sang. (WAVERLEY)

IN 1817 Scott reviewed anonymously in the *Quarterly Review* the first series of his *Tales of My Landlord*[1] and had this to say about his early novels:

'Our author has told us it was his object to present a succession of scenes and characters connected with Scotland in its past and present state, and we must own that his stories are so slightly constructed as to remind us of the showman's thread with which he draws up his pictures and presents them successively to the eye of the spectator. He seems seriously to have proceeded on Mr Bays's maxim – 'what the deuce is a plot good for, but to bring in fine things?' – Probability and perspicuity of narrative are sacrificed with the utmost indifference to the desire of producing effect; and provided the author can but contrive to 'surprize and elevate', he appears to think that he has done his duty to the public. Against this slovenly indifference we have already remonstrated, and we again enter our protest. It is in justice to the author himself that we do so, because, whatever merit individual scenes and passages may possess, (and none has been more ready than ourselves to offer our applause,) it is clear that their effect would be greatly enhanced by being disposed in a clear and continued narrative. We are the more earnest in this matter, because it seems that the author errs chiefly from carelessness. There may be something of system in it however: for we have remarked, that with an attention which amounts even to affectation, he has avoided the common language of narrative, and thrown his story, as much as possible, into a dramatic shape. In many cases this has added greatly to the effect, by keeping both the actors and action continually before the reader, and

placing him, in some measure, in the situation of the audience
at a theatre, who are compelled to gather the meaning of the
scene from what the dramatis personae say to each other, and
not from any explanation addressed immediately to themselves.
But though the author gains this advantage, and thereby
compels the reader to think of the personages of the novel and
not of the writer, yet the practice, especially pushed to the
extent we have noticed, is a principal cause of the flimsiness and
incoherent texture of which his greatest admirers are compelled
to complain . . .

In addition to the loose and incoherent style of the narration,
another leading fault in these novels is the total want of interest
which the reader attaches to the character of the hero. Waverley,
Brown, or Bertram in *Guy Mannering*, and Lovel in the *Antiquary*, are all brethren of a family; very amiable and very insipid
sort of young men. We think we can perceive that this error is
also in some degree occasioned by the dramatic principle upon
which the author frames his plots. His chief characters are never
actors, but always acted upon by the spur of circumstances, and
have their fates uniformly determined by the agency of the
subordinate persons.[2]

Scott's view of his novels has been taken by many — the
view that the Waverley novels are shapeless and confused,
but that in writing them Scott sometimes struck off happy
things, such as 'Wandering Willie's Tale', or Muckle-
backit's lament for his drowned son, or Jeanie Dean's
interview with the Queen, which (perhaps) make it worth
our while to wade through the tedium and incoherence of
much else. Scott in this review and in the novels encouraged the opinion that his stories were haphazard affairs
and had nothing to do with art. We know that he wrote
very fast, and this (illogically) confirms us in our view that
his novels cannot possibly contain any grand design.
Scott can, of course, be careless in the details of his
plots: it is impossible to understand how Rashleigh gains

financial power over Frank's father in *Rob Roy*; and in *Waverley* the sequence of events between Waverley's rescue on the road to Stirling and his arrival in Edinburgh is described with slipshod indifference. But as we reach the last page of *Waverley* what impresses most is the narrative energy of the novel to which everything has contributed, the sense of a 'unified total movement in which meaning chiefly lies'.[3] It is from this powerful impression of unity that criticism must begin. What Scott does, half in earnest, half in jest, in the passage just quoted, and what many readers do today, is to be false to this total impression, or to become so irritated by the slowness of the narrative in the first twenty-four chapters that they fail to see it and then judge the novel by rules that do not apply. Miss Tompkins says this:

> It is abundantly clear that careful articulation of plot and due regard for proportion, even in a simple story, were not among the principles of composition current in the 'seventies and 'eighties. But principles of composition there must have been; and we shall appreciate them more easily if, remembering the *Sentimental Journey* and *The Man of Feeling*, we discard the term structure with its architectural suggestions, and think of these books rather in terms of colour ... Plot, the chain of ordered and interconnected happenings, which became indispensable in the nineteenth century, has not yet established such an ascendancy over their minds, and the gist of their novels is often best expressed in terms of contrasted sentiment or of mental development.[4]

And, referring to an episode in a novel of the period which might not seem to have any function in the story, Miss Tompkins suggests that this episode 'has its place, not in the plot, but in the chiaroscuro of the story'. This is all apt. We do not need to discard the term 'structure', but we must recognise that there are more structures than one. It is easy to point out how unoriginal Scott was in his views on novel-writing. In the set-piece of Flora with her

harp by the waterfall in chapter 22 Scott gives an example
of that 'delineation of landscape and figure in the terms of
the picturesque' which was a common feature in fiction
towards the end of the eighteenth century. The scene
shows Scott at his worst ('Indeed the wild feeling of
romantic delight with which he heard the few first notes
she drew from her instrument amounted almost to a sense
of pain') and comes oddly after the gentle mockery of the
first chapter where Scott considers what title to give his
novel. 'Or if I had rather chosen to call my work a
"Sentimental Tale", would it not have been a sufficient
presage of a heroine with a profusion of auburn hair, and
a harp . . .' John Adolphus lists a number of other
theatrical scenes in Scott and remarks: 'As the beauty of
these tales is often enhanced by their admirable dramatic
effect, so too they occasionally lose in elegance and
simplicity by an over-ambitious seeking after what are
technically called *coups de théâtre* . . . the scene when
fully developed appears not properly dramatic but melo-
dramatic.'[5] Because *Waverley* is the first of Scott's
novels we should expect it to lean more heavily than the
others on the usual fictional techniques of the time. Scott
in the anonymous review concedes much to the critics,
but not everything. He insists that the novels have 'a
dramatic shape', but we cannot know if he means by this
anything more than Adolphus's phrase 'dramatic effect'.
In *Waverley* there is the same cavalier disregard for construction, for art, for the professional approach. 'Shall this
be a long or a short chapter? . . . I shall . . . proceed in my
story with all the brevity that my natural style of composition, partaking of what scholars call the periphrastic
and ambagitory, and the vulgar the circumbendibus, will
permit me' (ch. 24). Scott has been taken at his own estimate; but in the review in the *Quarterly* he gives signs that

the novel has an organisation, and in one place rounds briefly on his critics.

The first five chapters have few supporters and from the first were condemned. For Jeffrey, 'The worst part of the book by far is that portion of the first volume which contains the history of the hero's residence in England',[6] and Lockhart records that this was a common opinion and one which he shared: 'When the first volume was completed. I still could not get myself to think much of the Waverley-Honour scenes; and in this I afterwards found that I sympathized with many.'[7] But Scott explicitly defends these chapters and in a note attached to the end of chapter 5 he writes: 'These Introductory Chapters have been a good deal censured as tedious and unnecessary. Yet there are circumstances recorded in them which the author has not been able to retract or cancel.' Because the novel for a time moves slowly we call its movement casual. Scott believes that these chapters have a function, that they contribute to the total shape, that is, the total meaning of the book. If we are to discover how *Waverley* impresses by its energy and seriousness we should glance at these first chapters.

Chapter 3 ('Education') and chapter 4 ('Castle-Building') describe in detail the disastrous effects of desultory self-indulgent reading on Edward Waverley. He uses books to satisfy his passion for day-dreams; he reads only for 'the gratification of his amusement' and follows no course of study; and this must be called disastrous because 'he foresaw not that he was losing for ever the opportunity of acquiring habits of firm and assiduous application, of gaining the art of controlling, directing and concentrating the powers of his mind for earnest investigation'. The pointlessness of this haphazard reading is insisted upon: 'And yet, knowing much that is common but to few, Edward Waverley might justly be considered as ignorant, since he knew little of what adds dignity to man.' The effect of such a régime becomes clear for the first time when the susceptible and romantic Waverley seems likely to make a goddess of Miss Cecilia Stubbs. His aunt Rachel swiftly intervenes, and as a result Edward becomes Captain Waverley, of Gardiner's regiment of dragoons, and is dispatched to their quarters at Dundee in the course of a month. This puts paid to the hopes of Miss Stubbs, who finds that all her charms 'were lost upon a young officer of dragoons who wore, for the first time, his gold-laced hat, jack-boots and broadsword'; and she is dismissed from Waverley's life and from the novel with these words:

> My history must here take leave of the fair Cecilia, who, like many a daughter of Eve, after the departure of Edward, and the dissipation of certain idle visions which she had adopted, quietly contented herself with a *pis-aller*, and gave her hand, at the distance of six months, to the aforesaid Jones, son of the Baronet's steward, and heir (no unfertile prospect) to a steward's fortune, besides the snug probability of succeeding to his father's office. (ch. 5)

Miss Stubbs is dismissed and Waverley departs for the North; but the narrative shape of the book leads us to a repetition of the scene on a larger scale. For at the end of the novel Waverley has lost Flora, and his 'idle visions' are dissipated; he contents himself with a *pis aller* (Rose Bradwardine) who will succeed to her father's estates. The consolation for the failure of idle visions is in both cases a snug security. Waverley and Cecilia Stubbs have the same end, make the same compromise and are dismissed in the same way. The novel's end is in its beginning. And as the affair with Cecilia Stubbs is the first result of Waverley's 'education', so the whole novel results, as the whole of *Mansfield Park* results, from a failure in mental and moral training. Miss Stubbs is the first and least of Waverley's infatuations – Flora Mac-Ivor and Jacobitism are the others – and relates them directly to the education described in chapters 3 and 4. His infatuation with Flora Mac-Ivor grows with his infatuation for Jacobitism – they cannot be separated – and they disappear together.

It is not, of course, all Waverley's fault that he is so susceptible. His family has done great deeds in the past; he has been fed from childhood on the heroic and romantic tales of his ancestors. He lives in the house where they lived and can walk by the side of Mirkwood-Mere.

> There stood, in former times, a solitary tower upon a rock almost surrounded by the water, which had acquired the name of the Strength of Waverley, because, in perilous times, it had often been the refuge of the family. There, in the wars of York and Lancaster, the last adherents of the Red Rose who dared to maintain her cause, carried on a harassing and predatory warfare, till the stronghold was reduced by the celebrated Richard of Gloucester. Here, too, a party of cavaliers long maintained themselves under Nigel Waverley, elder brother of that William whose fate Aunt Rachel commemorated. Through these scenes it was that Edward loved to 'chew the cud of sweet and bitter fancy', and, like a child among his toys, culled and arranged, from the splendid yet useless imagery and emblems with which his imagination was stored, visions as brilliant and as fading as those of an evening sky. (ch. 4)

The words define for us Scott's attitude towards Jacobitism and the '45 as well as towards Waverley. The House of Waverley has always been on the losing side and we expect to find it on the losing side again. But there is a distinction to be made between the earlier allegiances and this one. The Royalist cause in the Civil War and the cause of the Red Rose were neither obviously lost causes at the time nor ultimately lost causes at all. But there is no excuse for not recognising the futility of this latest cause (whatever its charm), and Waverley's adherence to it comes, we are told, from an 'aberration from sound judgement'. Flora Mac-Ivor is the most intelligent person in the novel. (She alone 'places' Waverley: 'He can admire the moon and quote a stanza from Tasso' (ch. 52).) In chapter 68 she thinks of her brother's approaching execution, the failure of the rebellion and her own much sharper failure to restrain her brother from the desperate attempt.

> '. . . there is a busy devil at my heart, that whispers – but it were madness to listen to it – that the strength of mind on which Flora prided herself has murdered her brother! . . . Oh that I could recollect that I had but once said to him, 'He that striketh with the sword shall die by the sword'; that I had but once said, Remain at home; reserve yourself, your vassals, your life, for enterprises within the reach of man. But oh, Mr Waverley, I spurred his fiery temper, and half of his ruin at least lies with his sister!'
>
> Edward . . . recalled to her the principles on which both thought it their duty to act, and in which they had been educated.
>
> 'Do not think I have forgotten them', she said, looking up with eager quickness; 'I do not regret his attempt, because it was wrong! Oh no! on that point I am armed; but because it was impossible it could end otherwise than thus.'

Flora makes again the point that the whole novel makes. Jacobitism is not wrong; it is merely impossible. The clock cannot be put back. The cause of the Mac-Ivors is, like themselves, 'splendid yet useless'; and when Scott calls these visions of Waverley 'as brilliant and as fading as those of an evening sky', we may recall that the scene where Waverley meets Flora with her harp, a scene which Scott makes as deliberately pictorial and romantic as possible ('Here, like one of those lovely forms which decorate the landscapes of Poussin, Waverley found Flora gazing on the waterfall'), and in which Flora and her attendant appear 'like inhabitants of another region', takes place, too, under an 'evening sky'. The whole chapter – so obviously a set-piece – is totally relevant to the novel. The deliberately picturesque, static quality is recalled in chapter 71 by the addition to the furnishings in the dining-parlour of Tully-Veolan: 'It was a large and spirited painting, representing Fergus Mac-Ivor and Waverley in their Highland dress, the scene a wild, rocky, and mountainous pass, down which the clan were descending in the background.' We are to see the glamour of Jacobitism in terms of 'splendid yet useless imagery and emblems'. And even in the detail of the writing, Scott, who is so seldom a symbolic writer, suggests one of the central interests of the novel in the details of description. Waverley is escorted to Flora by her companion, Una.

> In a spot, about a quarter of a mile from the castle, two brooks, which formed the little river, had their junction. The larger of the two came down the long bare valley, which extended, apparently without any change or elevation of character, as far as the hills which formed its boundary permitted the eye to reach. But the other stream, which had its source among the mountains on the left hand of the strath, seemed to issue from a very narrow and dark opening betwixt two large rocks. These streams were different also in character. The larger was placid, and even sullen in its course, wheeling in deep eddies, or sleeping in dark blue pools; but the motions of the lesser brook were rapid and furious, issuing from between precipices, like a maniac from his confinement, all foam and uproar.
>
> It was up the course of this last stream that Waverley, like a knight of romance, was conducted by the fair Highland damsel, his silent guide. (ch. 22)

It is not possible to miss the identification of the 'rapid and furious' brook with rebellion that is about to burst from the mountains, nor the larger stream, 'placid and sleeping' with the House of Hanover; and in the expression 'like a maniac' Scott suggests (though less sharply than with the character of Peter Peebles in *Redgauntlet*) that militant Jacobitism is madness.

In chapter 2 we learn that Waverley's father and uncle had quarrelled and that his father had 'adopted a political creed more consonant both to reason and his own interest than the hereditary faith of Sir Everard in High Church and in the house of Stewart'. In the novel it is this everyday world which will re-assert itself and a creed 'more consonant both to reason and his own interest' which will influence Waverley in politics and love. The novel takes Waverley's politics and love together; each enforces the other, and early in the book Rose Bradwardine's qualities are shown to be destructive of romance:

> Besides, Rose Bradwardine, beautiful and amiable as we have described her, had not precisely the sort of beauty or merit, which captivates a romantic imagination in early youth. She was too frank, too confiding, too kind; amiable qualities, undoubtedly, but destructive of the marvellous, with which a youth of imagination delights to dress the empress of his affections. (ch. 14)

Scott's gently contemptuous irony is plain, and the total shape of the novel is the reversal of Waverley's romantic susceptibilities in all areas of his experience.

The question of education (what has been learnt and what must be unlearned) is central to the novel. The whole movement of the book shows this dramatically, but Scott makes the point explicitly as well. After the skirmish at Clifton, Waverley is separated from the Highland army and finds shelter for a time at the house of a young farmer.[8] In the weeks that followed 'he felt himself entitled to say firmly, though perhaps with a sigh, that the romance of

his life was ended, and that its real history had now commenced' (ch. 60). The closing scenes of the novel, the
execution of Vich Ian Vohr and Evan Maccombich, the
snug marriage settlement with Rose Bradwardine, are in
different ways an emphasis on 'real history'.

The opening chapters, then, deserve Scott's defence of
them. The question of education is raised; the question of
politics, Whig and Tory, is discussed and shown to be
inseparable from education; and, in the episode of Miss
Cecilia Stubbs, Scott gives us in his typical narrative way
the first of many apparently trivial and irrelevant episodes
which are, however, essential parts of the narrative and
focus our attention on the main narrative line (or meaning) of the novel. There is something else in these opening chapters – something that leads to the heart of the
novel.

The narrative reaches easily and inevitably its sharpest
focus in a scene which makes clear the essential shape or
structure of *Waverley*. W. P. Ker said of *Waverley* that
'Scott gets very near to the tension of tragedy, but never
quite uses it',[9] and Alexander Welsh endorses the remark.
But to consider the novel in terms of tragedy is irrelevant;
we should think of it as an elegy. This sharpest point of
focus is reached in chapters 63 and 65. In chapter 63
('Desolation') Waverley comes for the second time in the
book to Tully-Veolan. As he approaches the house he
recalls his former happy visit, and Scott tells us of his
'feelings and sentiments – how different from those which
attended his first entrance!' We recall the earlier description in chapter 8 of Tully-Veolan in its prosperity and are
impressed by how far we, like Waverley, have travelled
'within the course of a very few months'. The contrasting
scenes offer us the distinctive shape of the book, and give
to the later description its elegiac note.

A single glance announced that great changes had taken place. One half of the gate, entirely destroyed, and split up for firewood, lay in piles, ready to be taken away; the other swung uselessly about upon its loosened hinges. The battlements above the gate were broken and thrown down, and the carved Bears, which were said to have done sentinel's duty upon the top for centuries, now, hurled from their posts, lay among the rubbish. The avenue was cruelly wasted. Several large trees were felled and left lying across the path; and the cattle of the villagers, and the more rude hoofs of dragoon horses, had poached into black mud the verdant turf which Waverley had so much admired.

Upon entering the courtyard, Edward saw the fears realised which these circumstances had excited. The place had been sacked by the King's troops, who, in wanton mischief, had even attempted to burn it; and though the thickness of the walls had resisted the fire, unless to a partial extent, the stables and out-houses were totally consumed. The towers and pinnacles of the main building were scorched and blackened; the pavement of the court broken and shattered; the doors torn down entirely, or hanging by a single hinge; the windows dashed in and demolished, and the court strewed with articles of furniture broken into fragments . . . The fountain was demolished, and the spring, which had supplied it, now flooded the courtyard. The stone basin seemed to be destined for a drinking-trough for cattle, from the manner in which it was arranged upon the ground. The whole tribe of Bears, large and small, had experienced as little favour as those at the head of the avenue, and one or two of the family pictures, which seemed to have served as targets for the soldiers, lay on the ground in tatters . . . When he entered upon the terrace, new scenes of desolation were visible. The balus-trade was broken down, the walls destroyed, the borders over-grown with weeds, and the fruit-trees cut down or grubbed up. In one compartment of this old-fashioned garden were two immense horse-chestnut trees, of whose size the Baron was particularly vain: too lazy, perhaps, to cut them down, the spoilers, with malevolent ingenuity, had mined them, and placed a quantity of gunpowder in the cavity. One had been shivered to pieces by the explosion, and the fragments lay scattered around, encumbering the ground it had so long shadowed. The other mine had been more partial in its effect. About one-fourth of the trunk of the tree was torn from the mass, which, mutilated and defaced on the one side, still spread on the other its ample and undiminished boughs. (ch. 63)

As Waverley surveys the scene he hears a voice singing a lament. It is daft Davie Gellatley. He cannot talk rationally, and all he can say to Waverley is 'A' dead and gane – a' dead and gane'. What Davie means by the words is made clear a few pages later when the Baron Bradwardine, in hiding on his estates from the English soldiery, comments on the whole reversal in fortunes.

A natural sigh closed the sentence; but the quiet equanimity with which the Baron endured his misfortunes, had something in it venerable and even sublime. There was no fruitless repining, no turbid melancholy; he bore his lot, and the hardships which it involved, with a good-humoured, though serious composure, and used no violent language against the prevailing party.

'I did what I thought my duty,' said the good old man, 'and questionless they are doing what they think theirs. It grieves me sometimes to look upon these blackened walls of the house of my ancestors; but doubtless officers cannot always keep the soldier's hand from depredation and spuilzie; and Gustavus Adolphus himself, as ye may read in Colonel Munro his Expedition with the worthy Scotch regiment called Mackay's regiment, did often permit it. – Indeed I have myself seen as sad sights as Tully-Veolan now is, when I served with the Marechal Duke of Berwick. To be sure we may say with Virgilius Maro, *Fuimus Troes* – and there's the end of an auld sang. But houses and families and men have a' stood lang eneugh when they have stood till they fall with honour; and now I hae gotten a house that is not unlike a *domus ultima*' – they were now standing below a steep rock. 'We poor Jacobites,' continued the Baron, looking up, 'are now like the conies in Holy Scripture (which the great traveller Pococke calleth Jerboa), a feeble people, that make our abode in the rocks.' (ch. 65)

The narrative shape of the book is here fully revealed. The passage is moving and impressive because of all that has gone before, but it prescribes how we shall see all that has gone before. Professor Davie comments well on the second extract and notes the elegiac quality:

> All this, by giving the nostalgic feeling something precise and articulated on which to work, takes the passage out of the realm of the nostalgic as commonly understood, and makes it elegiac, something of a stately ritual, clear-sighted, composed, and sad rather than melancholy – like the state of mind of the Baron himself.[10]

Scott achieves this note, this dignity, without relaxing the emphasis on the gentle pedantry of the Baron. And after the singing of the 'Border Widow's Lament' a few pages earlier by David Gellatley the phrase 'the end of an auld sang' comes with perfect rightness. For this is what the novel records: 'the end of an auld sang'. What the Baron laments is not only the laying waste of Tully-Veolan, but the destruction of an older way of life; and it is this larger meaning which gives these chapters their resonance. Scott nowhere suggests that the military defeat of the '45 was responsible for this loss of an older culture, though David Craig seems to think that he does.[11] The '45 in this novel is used to dramatise the passing of something that would have passed in any case; it focuses the elegiac quality.[12] The words 'the end of an auld sang' have their aptness and power to move us because the whole novel has been directed towards them; they have, when they come, the whole impetus of the book behind them. The change to a world where traditional values and social patterns have broken down has been stressed from the beginning, and Scott extends it beyond the borders of Scotland. In the opening chapters the deeds of Wilibert of Waverley in the Holy Land contrast with Waverley's father who 'read his recantation at the beginning of his career, and entered life as an avowed Whig and friend of the Hanoverian succession'. When Waverley leaves for Scotland he is accompanied by only two domestics.

> 'You will depart with but a small retinue,' quoth the Baronet, 'compared to Sir Hildebrand, when he mustered before the gate of the Hall a larger body of horse than your whole regiment consists of. I could have wished that these twenty young fellows from my estate, who have enlisted in your troop, had been to march with you on your journey to Scotland. It would have been something, at least; but I am told their attendance would be thought unusual in these days when every new and foolish fashion is introduced to break the natural dependence of the people upon their landlords.' (ch. 6)

We learn that instead of being able to rely on this 'natural dependence', Sir Everard has had to encourage these twenty young fellows with a bribe. When Baron Brad-wardine's cows are rustled in chapter 15, he recalls how a hundred years earlier his grandsire had been able to levy two hundred horse within his own bounds in pursuit of five hundred highland reivers.

Waverley, however, is not just an elegy, a lament that the old order is changing; it is something far more interesting and complex. 'The elegiac presents a herosim unspoiled by irony', remarks Northrop Frye,[13] and the real emotional importance to Scott and us of the death of this older world is checked by the 'ironic qualifications' that Scott insists upon. To describe the whole movement of the novel as one of 'progressive enchantment and dis-enchantment'[14] is to describe merely Waverley's own development and not our experience as readers. The novel is great because Scott can go beyond a full appreciation of what has been lost and can note with equal care its present impossibility and even absurdity. We can see how much we must qualify the word *elegiac* as a description of the mood of the book by going back again to the picture of the destruction of Tully-Veolan, a destruction that is more than the desolation of one country house. But the novel does not rest here. In chapter 71 we are given a final picture of Tully-Veolan, repaired and restored, with 'every mark of devastation . . . already totally obliterated'. The house is once again as it was when Waverley first saw it. For a moment we may even think that what has been lost has come again. But the repairing of the building merely emphasises the destruction of what cannot be repaired. Bailie Macwheeble can gloat that 'Mr Bradwardine, your family estate is your own once more in full property'. But Tully-Veolan has been purchased from the wretched Malcom Bradwardine of Inch-Grabbit by an Englishman, Colonel Talbot, and bought from him by another Englishman, Edward Waverley; and something of Scott's complex reaction to this change is suggested with dry amusement by the one addition to the furniture of the restored dining parlour, the picture of Edward Waverley and Fergus Mac-Ivor in their Highland dress. We cannot forget that as they dine the clan of Mac-Ivor is dispersed and at the mercy of the English army, and the head of Vich Ian Vohr rots above the Scotch Gate at Carlisle.

The final chapters, with the restoration of Tully-Veolan and the marriage of Waverley to Rose Bradwardine are part of the ironic qualification that gives the novel its distinctive shape. The ironic qualifications of the elegiac theme (some other examples will be noticed shortly) are the novel's structure. The book ends 'happily'; but it is a local happiness that merely emphasises the book's very different conclusion. We never feel that the happy ending contradicts 'the end of an auld sang', or that the end is other than right. If Scott had ended at the execution of

Vich Ian Vohr, the novel would have been different; but he does not finish what he wants to say until the last page. The conventional happy ending is a fine example of Scott's taking a standard and fortuitous device from fiction and making it essential to the meaning of the novel, making it the inevitable point towards which the whole novel has been directed. The sense that we have come to 'the end of an auld sang' is even stronger at the end of this book than it was during the Baron's lament. At that point the old world seemed to have been destroyed gloriously ('But houses and families and men have a' stood lang eneugh when they have stood till they fall with honour'). The Baron has throughout the book been shown as 'the very model of the old Scottish cavalier, with all his excellencies and peculiarities. It is a character, Captain Waverley, which is fast disappearing.' He slips out of the story, humoured by everyone, and all that we hear of is the ten thousand a year that Rose will have as Lady Waverley, and Bailie Macwheeble (the lawyer now, appropriately, at the centre of things) and his 'wee bit minute of an ante-nuptial contract, *intuitu matrimonii*, so it cannot be subject to reduction hereafter, as a donation *inter virum et uxorem*'. We are back with Miss Cecilia Stubbs and her marriage to the son of Sir Everard's steward.

This anti-climax, or ironic qualification, which is the essential shape of the book, is repeated on a smaller scale in other places. In chapter 69 Waverley visits Vich Ian Vohr (Glennaquoich) for the last time, and we see the chief at his finest – stoical, selfless and dignified. The next morning, after the execution, Waverley leaves Carlisle with his servant Alick Polwarth, who gives the last word in the book on Fergus: 'It's a great pity of Evan Dhu, who was a very weel-meaning, good-natured man, to be a Hielandman; and indeed so was the Laird o' Glennaquoich

too, for that matter when he wasna in ane o' his tirrivies.'
This is the sort of comment, placed where it is, that made
many early readers of Scott compare him with Shakespeare. Its aim is the aim of the whole book: to recognise
the worth of old-fashioned heroism and to look away from
it to the 'quiet virtues' (the phrase is used of Rose Bradwardine by Flora Mac-Ivor), which alone are required in
the present. If Polwarth's comment reminds readers of
Falstaff, this will be apt, since this novel (like Scott's
other novels considered in this book) is concerned with
the nature of Honour. Consideration of the word 'Honour'
explains the presence of some episodes in the book and
throws light on Scott's remark that the author of *Waverley* 'has thrown his story into a dramatic shape'.

'Waverley-Honour', we learn in chapter 2, is the name
of Edward's ancestral home, and the name is justified. For
centuries it has been the home of 'ancient manners and
primitive integrity'; the family motto is *Sans tache* and
'honour and generosity were hereditary attributes of the
house of Waverley'. When Sir Everard was a young man
he made a visit 'to a noble peer on the confines of the shire
of untainted descent, steady Tory principles, and the
happy father of six unmarried and accomplished daugh-
ters', and he decided in favour of the youngest. When he
learnt that her affections were already fixed, 'with a grace
and delicacy worthy of the hero of a romance, Sir Everard
withdrew his claim to the hand of Lady Emily'. It is no
longer possible for a young man to face all situations like
a hero of romance, and Scott's gently ironic and dismissive tone here suggests the simplicity and old-fashioned-
ness of this sort of honour. The passive and indecisive
nature of Waverley, and the half-pun on his name have
been noticed since the novel first appeared. The *Quarterly
Review* noticed the 'vacillating and dilatory propensity of

his mind'[15] and in his own anonymous review of *Tales of My Landlord* Scott refers to Waverley 'as a reed blown about at the pleasure of every breeze'.[16] In the novel other people make the same discovery about the hero: 'You are blown about with every kind of doctrine', says Fergus. And twice in the novel there is deliberate punning on his name. In chapter 7 Scott tells us of Edward's 'wavering and unsettled habit of mind', and in chapter 25 we are given a quotation from a London journal which refers to Waverley's father and adds: 'we understand that this same Richard who hath done all this is not the only example of the *Wavering Honour* of W-v-r-l-y H-n-r'. Waverley is a wavering hero not simply because he flirts with Jacobitism (that is, with Romance) while in the service of the House of Hanover, but because in him Scott dramatises his own awareness of the changing meaning of 'Honour' in a changing world. And this changing meaning of 'Honour', which is the sharpest way of pointing to the changes which make all attempts to put the clock back futile, is shown in a number of scenes which seem in terms of plot to be away from the centre of the novel.[17]

In chapter 11 Waverley, on the day of his arrival at Tully-Veolan, has a merry evening with his host and two neighbours. Too much wine is drunk, and one of the neighbours, the Laird of Balmawhapple, proposes the toast of 'the little gentleman in black velvet'. Waverley does not fully understand the reference, 'yet felt inclined to take umbrage at a toast which seemed . . . to have a peculiar and uncivil reference to the Government which he served'. Waverley wishes to reply, but Baron Bradwardine takes Waverley's quarrel upon himself. The following morning Waverley recalls the quarrel with dissatisfaction.

He had received a personal affront, – he, a gentleman, a soldier
and a Waverley. True, the person who offered it was not, at the
time it was given, possessed of the moderate share of sense which
nature had allotted him; true also, in resenting this insult, he
would break the laws of Heaven, as well as of his country; true,
in doing so, he might take the life of a young man who perhaps
respectably discharged the social duties, and render his family
miserable; or he might lose his own; – no pleasant alternative
even to the bravest, when it is debated coolly and in private.

All this pressed on his mind; yet the original statement re-
curred with the same irresistible force. He had received a personal
insult; he was of the House of Waverley; and he bore a com-
mission. There was no alternative . . . (ch. 12)

The duel must take place. This is the hero's first adventure in Scotland, and Scott's irony is obvious as he gives
us Waverley's reactions to the insult he had received from
Balmawhapple. Scott makes plain the foolishness of the
traditional code of honour in respect of duelling, and
relates it to Waverley's adoption of Jacobitism. Waverley
imagines that he has received an insult from his command-
ing officer. He will be breaking the laws of his country by
joining the Prince's standard, and he may take the lives
of others, or even lose his own. But all this 'Reason' cannot compete with an outdated and over-simple code of
honour. In chapter 40 Waverley meets and is flattered by
the Prince: 'Rejected, slandered, and threatened upon the
one side, he was irresistibly attracted to the cause which
the prejudices of education, and the political principles of
his family, had already recommended as the most just.
These thoughts rushed through his mind like a torrent...'
This later episode echoes and explains the earlier one.

Baron Bradwardine represents all that is finest in the
old order.[18] Flora Mac-Ivor calls him 'the very model of
the old Scottish cavalier with all his excellencies and
peculiarities. "It is a character, Captain Waverley, which

is fast disappearing; for its best point was a self-respect which was never lost sight of till now.'' Scott gives him all his sympathy, but is concerned as much with his 'peculiarities' as with his 'excellencies'. The peculiarity is strikingly there in the Baron's concern with the hereditary service or feudal homage, traditionally performed by the representative of the house of Bradwardine, of removing the King's boots. For the Baron this is a matter of great moment, and he succeeds in performing this ceremony for Prince Charles. The account of this in the gazette reads:

> in the meanwhile, his Royal Highness, in his father's name and authority, has been pleased to grant him an honourable aug-mentation to his paternal coat of arms, being a budget or boot-jack, disposed saltier-wise with a naked broadsword, to be borne in the dexter cantle of the shield; and, as an additional motto, on a scroll beneath, the words, 'Draw and draw off.'

This episode, and Waverley's thoughts on duelling, are further ironic qualifications which illuminate the chang-ing notion of 'Honour', a change that is a part of the much larger changes which the novel records, regrets and accepts. Scott describes the incident of removing the Prince's shoes as 'an episode in respect to the principal story', and means by this that it is irrelevant. In fact it is an important piece in the total organisation of the novel, in the total narrative that defines and dramatises Scott's own attitude towards the past. As with every other episode, it makes the novel something very different from an essay in nostalgia.

Chapter 22 contains the set-piece already referred to, with Flora and Waverley at the waterfall. In the next chapter they are joined by Fergus and an impossibly 'precious' conversation follows which for most readers is the weakest and most tiresome thing in the book.

'A Truce, dear Fergus! spare us those most tedious and insipid persons of all Arcadia. Do not, for Heaven's sake, bring down Coridon and Lindor upon us.'

'Nay, if you cannot relish *la houlette et le chalumeau*, have with you in heroic strains.'

This is a sample. In chapter 28 Waverley decides to go to Edinburgh in an attempt to establish his innocence with the Government. He is accompanied as far as the nearest market town by Callum Beg, a member of the clan Mac-Ivor, and at the sign of the Seven-branched Golden Candlestick they meet the inn-keeper, Mr Ebenezer Cruickshanks, who interrogates Callum Beg in this fashion:

'Ye'll be frae the north, young man?'
'And ye may say that,' answered Callum.
'And ye'll hae ridden a lang way the day, it may weel be?'
'Sae lang, that I could weel tak a dram.'
'Gudwife, bring the gill stoup . . .'
'Ye'll no hae mickle better whisky than that aboon the Pass?'
'I'm nae frae aboon the Pass.'
'Ye're a Highlandman by your tongue?'
'Na; I am but just Aberdeen-a-way . . .'
'Aweel, Duncan – did you say your name was Duncan, or Donald?'
'Na, man – Jamie – Jamie Steenson – I telt ye before.'

Scott's gifts for comedy and for reproducing low-life speech have always been recognised. But the effect of this dialogue is something more; it gives to the earlier high-falutin', 'literary' talk of Fergus and Flora and Waverley a remoteness from reality that is a part of their meaning as characters in the novel. (We recall that Flora and her companion had seemed, at the waterfall, 'like inhabitants of another region'.)

The horse that Waverley hires from Ebenezer Cruick-shanks throws a shoe, and Waverley goes to the black-smith in the village of Cairnvreckan to have it replaced. The villagers are agitated and excited by the rumours of an imminent descent by the Highlanders, and Waverley is anxious for information.

Ere Waverley could ask particulars, a strong, large-boned, hard-featured woman, about forty, dressed as if her clothes had been flung on with a pitchfork, her cheeks flushed with a scarlet red where they were not smutted with soot and lamp-black, jostled through the crowd, and, brandishing high a child of two years old, which she danced in her arms, without regard to its screams of terror, sang forth, with all her might, –

'Charlie is my darling, my darling, my darling,
Charlie is my darling,
The young Chevalier!'

'D'ye hear what's come ower ye now', continued the virago, 'ye whingeing Whig carles? D'ye hear wha's coming to cow yer cracks? . . .'

'And that's a' your Whiggery', re-echoed the Jacobite heroine; 'that's a' your Whiggery, and your presbytery, ye cut-lugged, graning carles! What! d'y think the lads wi' the kilts will care for yer synods and yer presbyteries, and yer buttock-mail, and yer stool o' repentance? . . .'

The furious, drunken, foolish Jacobite loyalty of the smith's wife makes us think again about the passionate loyalty of Flora Mac-Ivor, and so has its part in the rhythm of the story. The method, again, is dramatic rather than narrative; the aim, again, is to show that tradi-tional notions of Honour have no meaning in a world that has changed. (Waverley, significantly, never fought the duel with Balmawhapple; it was fought on his behalf by the Baron Bradwardine.) For the last representative of 'Waverley-Honour' there is to be no heroic death, but the happy cosiness of marriage and the good things of life.

For Scott this is the inevitable end; any other conclusion
would be anachronistic, and all the detail of the book has
pointed this way. But the ironic qualifications are no more
the full meaning of the novel than is Scott's elegiac awareness of a passing way of life. Waverley survives, but many
other better people do not; and these others, in their
dying, make Waverley's life unavoidably shoddy. Houghton, who followed Waverley from England, is wounded
in a skirmish shortly before the battle of Prestonpans and
is left to die by the Highlanders when he will say nothing
about the strength of his regiment. Colonel Gardiner, a
good man, who commanded the regiment from which
Waverley deserted, fights heroically at Prestonpans and is
killed by the blow of a scythe. (We recall Waverley's fear
– rapidly overcome – that in the duel with Balmawhapple
he might 'take the life of a young man who perhaps
respectably discharged the social duties, and render his
family miserable'.) Houghton and Colonel Gardiner behave with bravery and honour. Vich Ian Vohr and Evan
Dhu Maccombich are taken prisoner and die with courage
and dignity. In contrast to these Waverley has life, but he
has it less abundantly.

Scott did not greatly care for Edward Waverley. 'The
hero is a sneaking piece of imbecility; and if he had
married Flora she would have set him up upon the
chimney piece.'[19] Even if our opinion of him is less sharp
we still find it hard to admire him. '"I cannot permit you,
Colonel Talbot," answered Waverley, "to speak of any
plan which turns on my deserting an enterprise in which
I have engaged hastily, but certainly voluntarily, and with
the purpose of abiding the issue"' (ch. 51). But Waverley
does desert the enterprise. If Waverley is a dull dog; if at
the end he willingly adopts (like his father) 'a political
creed more consonant both to reason and his own interest

than the hereditary faith', we must recognise that, like other Scott heroes, he has the essential ability to reject a past, not because it is wrong but because it is impossible. He survives. He is the new hero who settles for Rose and safety. The marriage is not a 'symbolic compromise'; it is not a compromise at all, but a total rejection of the past. Our impression of Waverley is our recognition of the price paid.

4 'A Legend of Montrose' and 'Rob Roy'

That fellow is formed to go through the world.

(*A Legend of Montrose*)

I

I N his *Letters to Richard Heber* John Adolphus makes a criticism which has often been repeated:

> It seems not improbable that the Legend of Montrose was, in part, formed out of materials originally collected for a metrical romance; but the author has succeeded ill in making this portion of his fable combine and harmonize with the rest. There appears a natural incongruity between the lofty and imaginative, and the broad and familiar parts of the subject; they may be joined, but they refuse to blend.[1]

This suggestion that the two elements in the novel, the tale of Allan M'Aulay and the Children of the Mist, and the story, or simply the character, of Dugald Dalgetty, have nothing to do with one another is fostered by Scott himself in the opening words of his Introduction:

> The *Legend of Montrose* was written chiefly with a view to place before the reader the melancholy fate of John Lord Kilpont, eldest son of William Earl of Airth and Menteith, and the singular circumstances attending the birth and history of James Stewart of Ardvoirlich, by whose hand the unfortunate nobleman fell.

This is intended as the main subject; but a little later Scott adds: 'The author has endeavoured to enliven the tragedy of the tale by the introduction of a personage [Dugald Dalgetty] proper to the time and country'. Dalgetty, however, is not simply there 'to enliven the tragedy'; it is, in fact, because of him that the tale is not a tragedy. He is the ironic observer of the 'lofty and imaginative' part; it is through him that we have Scott's consistent ironic qualification of the romantic and the glamorous. Scott in his Introduction admits his liking for Dalgetty, but is afraid that 'he has fallen into the error of assigning to the Captain too prominent a part in the story'. And then he quotes from a criticism in the *Edinburgh Review* that endorses this opinion:

> There is too much, perhaps, of Dalgetty, – or, rather, he engrosses too great a proportion of the work, – for, in himself, we think he is uniformly entertaining; – and the author has nowhere shown more affinity to that matchless spirit who could bring out his Falstaffs and his Pistols, in act after act, and play after play, and exercise them every time with scenes of unbounded loquacity, without either exhausting their humour, or varying a note from its characteristic tone, than in his large and reiterated specimens of the eloquence of the redoubted Rittmaster.

No modern reader is likely to complain that there is too much of Dalgetty; and it is odd that, even with the reference to Falstaff, we do not see that Dalgetty's role, like Falstaff's, is not to provide comic relief, but to comment on and 'place' the actions of others: 'In other words, though Falstaff is, to quote Professor Muir, "a living criticism of the world of *policy*," satirizing the gulf between precept and practice in the world of rank, he has anything but the last word on the values of life.'[2] Dugald Dalgetty has not 'the last word on the values of life' either; we cannot fail to recognize the limitations of his worldly wisdom. But, like Steenie Steenson in *Redgauntlet*, he is the success-

ful man, and the consistent critic of the heroics and
romance of the novel. 'Parasitical, he yet gives to life as
much as he takes, and indeed provides amidst all his
vices a vast salutary criticism of the world of war and
policy.'[3] The two parts of the novel form a unity since we
see the 'lofty and imaginative' part largely through Dalgetty's eyes.

Dalgetty is handled more harshly in the Introduction
than in the novel. In the Introduction he is seen only as a
mercenary soldier:

> A cavalier of honour, in search of his fortune, might, for
> example, change his service as he would his shirt, fight, like the
> doughty Captain Dalgetty, in one cause after another, without
> regard to the justice of the quarrel, and might plunder the
> peasantry subjected to him by the fate of war with the most
> unrelenting rapacity . . .

But in the novel the target is rather different. 'The gay
cavaliers of Whitehall', Montrose remarks, 'are as great
self-seekers as our friend Dalgetty.' After the massacre at
Inverlochy Annot Lyle sees that on the battlefield 'the
spoilers were busy tearing the clothes from the victims of
war and feudal ambition, with as much indifference as if
they had not been of the same species . . .' and these
spoilers are not mercenaries but Highlanders. Dalgetty,
as a soldier of fortune, may not care which side he fights
for; but the novel reminds us that Montrose, Sir John
Hurry and the 'hero' of the novel, Menteith, have changed
sides too.

Scott likes and admires Dalgetty, but the tone of the
Introduction sometimes creeps into the novel; when it
does, the sharp comments on Dalgetty usually rebound on
the head of the commentator. To glance at one or two
places where Dalgetty is harshly handled is to see something of his function in the narrative structure of the

novel. The first place is early in the novel (chapter 4) shortly after Lord Menteith and Montrose (disguised as Menteith's servant and travelling under the name of Anderson) have encountered the formidably armed Dalgetty and have had their first sample of his pedantry and aplomb.

> 'I differ from you, Anderson', said Lord Menteith; 'I think this fellow Dalgetty is one of those horse-leeches, whose appetite for blood being only sharpened by what he has sucked in foreign countries, he is now returned to batten upon that of his own. Shame on the pack of these mercenary swordmen! they have made the name of Scot through all Europe equivalent to that of a pitiful mercenary, who knows neither honour nor principle but his month's pay, who transfers his allegiance from standard to standard, at the pleasure of fortune or the highest bidder . . .'

Towards the end of the novel Menteith again comments on Dalgetty, now dubbed a knight by Montrose:

> 'There goes the hound,' said Menteith, 'breaking the face, and trampling on the body, of many a better man than himself; and as eager on his sordid spoil as a vulture that stoops upon carrion. Yet this man the world calls a soldier – and you, my lord, select him as worthy of the honours of chivalry, if such they can at this day be termed. You have made the collar of knighthood the decoration of a mere bloodhound.' (ch. 20)

We accept Menteith's earlier comment because we have then hardly met Dalgetty, and Menteith urges the usual objections to mercenary soldiers. With Menteith's second comment our sympathies are all with Dalgetty; for by then we have seen too many other 'mere bloodhounds' (Ranald of the Mist, Allan M'Aulay) who know 'neither honour nor principle'. Once again, the novel examines the notion of 'Honour'.

Captain Dugald Dalgetty is a Lowlander; after many

years of service in continental armies he is almost a foreigner to his native land, and is completely a foreigner
among the Highlanders, both the humble and the well-
born, of the story. He is the travelling observer. We meet
him first on horseback, detached and alone (he has neither
family nor political ties) and able to look coolly at the
political problems and factions of Scotland that are erupt-
ing into civil war. 'I am for God and my standard' are his
opening words when challenged to declare himself and the
cause he supports.

> 'I should have thought,' answered the gentleman [Menteith],
> 'that, when loyalty and religion are at stake, no gentleman or
> man of honour could be long in choosing his party.'
>
> 'Truly, sir,' replied the trooper, '. . . I am ready to prove to
> ye *logice*, that my resolution to defer, for a certain season, the
> taking upon me either of these quarrels, not only becometh me
> as a gentleman and a man of honour, but also as a person of
> sense and prudence, one imbued with humane letters in his
> early youth . . .' (ch. 2)

This reply is central to *A Legend of Montrose*; the question
of Honour is raised at once, and Dalgetty's insistence
that he, too, is 'man of honour' makes plain that the novel
will contrast opposing notions of Honour, feudal and
modern (as, in *Redgauntlet*, Wandering Willie, Crosbie
and Redgauntlet show the clash of opposing meanings of
the word) and through this contrast will dramatise the
clash of different cultures. Honour for Dalgetty, as for
Alan Fairford and Wandering Willie, is associated with
sense and prudence; these qualities make it possible for
Dalgetty and Wandering Willie's 'gudesire' to survive
political change. They are successful men and there is
nothing dishonourable in their success.

Only in *A Legend of Montrose* are the hero and the chief
comic character the same person, and this not only gives

to the novel much of its energy and drive, but enables Scott to have his usual peripatetic 'hero-observer', whose wanderings, as in *Redgauntlet, Old Mortality, Waverley* and *Rob Roy* are not so much geographical as sociological. The Scott 'hero' generally finds himself in a more primitive society that observes a narrow loyalty or nationalism. In *A Legend of Montrose* the energy that Scott can always give to his comic characters (in this case Dalgetty) adds force to the contrast between the two ways of life and to the commentary that Dalgetty makes on the older of these.

Dalgetty is the only comic character in the book; the narrative structure is simpler and is indicated by his introduction to the Royalist cause, his subsequent journey to the remote West and his final extrication from both. When we first meet Dalgetty in chapter 2, he seems likely to take up arms against the King, and he talks at length of his continental service and of his repeated changes of side. The conventional dishonour of his mercenary calling is stressed; Lord Menteith (as we saw) is shocked, and our own reaction is possibly one of contempt. At the end of the novel Dalgetty changes sides once more, but Scott has by now successfully asked the questions: What is Honour? Which is preferable, the time-serving of Dalgetty or the antiquated and savage notions of aristocratic Honour that are displayed for us so damningly throughout the book?

Dalgetty, then, is the detached observer, and his critical role and good sense are made quite clear by Scott:

> 'Ye speak reasonably, my lord', said Dalgetty, 'and *ceteris paribus*, I might be induced to see the matter in the same light. But, my lord, there is a southern proverb, – fine words butter no parsnips. I have heard enough since I came here, to satisfy me that a cavalier of honour is free to take any part in this civil

embroilment whilk he may find most convenient for his own peculiar. Loyalty is your password, my lord – Liberty, roars another chield from the other side of the strath – the King, shouts one war-cry – the Parliament roars another – Montrose, for ever, cries Donald, waving his bonnet – Argyle and leven, cries a south-country Saunders, vapouring with his hat and feather. Fight for the bishops, says a priest, with his gown and rochet – Stand stout for the Kirk, cries a minister, in a Geneva cap and band. – Good watchwords all – excellent watchwords. Whilk cause is the best I cannot say. But sure am I, that I have fought knee-deep in blood many a day for one that was ten degrees worse than the worst of them all.' (ch. 3)

Dalgetty identifies 'Honour' with 'Interest':

'And pray, Captain Dalgetty,' said his lordship, 'since the pretensions of both parties seem to you so equal, will you please to inform us by what circumstances your preference will be determined?'

'Simply upon two considerations, my lord,' answered the soldier. 'Being, first, on which side my services would be in most honourable request; – And, secondly, whilk is a corollary of the first, by whilk party they are likely to be most gratefully requited.' (ch. 3)

And Scott points again ironically to a meaning of 'Honour' with Dalgetty's comment, 'wherefore these valiant Irishes, being all put to the sword, as is usual in such cases, did nevertheless gain immortal praise and honour . . .'

Montrose recognises that Dalgetty, a mercenary soldier, is a man of the times and that without him they would hardly be able to carry on their enterprise. But Scott has not only to persuade us that Dalgetty is necessary, but to make him a sympathetic figure. Much of the sympathy and regard we feel for him comes from the earthy good-sense that he often shows. At one point he is

afraid (with reason) that as the envoy of Montrose he may
be executed by Argyle:

> 'By my honour, Captain Dalgetty,' said Montrose, 'should
> the Marquis, contrary to the rules of war, dare to practise any
> atrocity against you, you may depend upon my taking such signal
> vengeance that all Scotland shall ring of it.'
> 'That will do but little for Dalgetty,' returned the captain . . .'
> (ch. 8)

'That fellow', said Sir Miles Musgrave, 'is formed to go
through the world.'

In chapter 10 Dalgetty departs (as Waverley departs
from Tully-Veolan) into the wild Highlands. Through
everything he preserves his indestructible aplomb, and
criticises, smugly but intelligently, what he sees. And
what he sees is an older way of life. He is unimpressed by
the Marquis of Argyle and the other great Highland
chiefs. (If he admires Montrose it is because he is
impressed by Montrose's ability as a soldier and not by
his rank.) He unglamourises the clans by seeing them,
detachedly, as the wildest of tribes: 'But yours is a pretty
irregular scythian kind of warfare, Ranald, much resem-
bling that of Turks, Tartars and other Asiatic people.'
The cruel behaviour of the Children of the Mist of putting bread into a dead man's mouth is not simply condemned as 'too wild and savage for civilized acceptance',
but as a wastage of good victuals. When Lord Menteith
asks Dalgetty to give him all the particulars he had heard
of the attack on Ardenvohr many years earlier and of the
escape of Sir Duncan's daughter, he is told:

> 'I will be your confessor, or assessor – either or both. No one
> can be so fit, for I had heard the whole story a month ago at
> Inverary Castle – but onslaughts like that of Ardenvohr confuse
> each other in my memory, which is besides occupied with
> matters of more importance.' (ch. 21)

This is the effect which the 'broad and familiar' part of the novel has on the 'lofty and imaginative': we consider it to be of 'more importance'. We and Dalgetty have seen the treachery of Argyle, the wildness of the Children of the Mist, the madness and savagery of Allan M'Aulay, the haughtiness of Lord Menteith, the feudalism of the Highland chiefs and the notions of Honour (shared by all) which are either absurd or insincere. (Montrose, who is intended, it seems, to represent the voice of moderation and good sense never comes alive in the novel – Colonel Talbot in *Waverley* is a more successful figure – and it is not Montrose but Dalgetty who dramatises for us the inadequacies of the characters in the novel and their civilisation.)

At the end of the novel Scott remarks that the *dramatis personae* have been limited. One way in which Scott achieves this limitation is by making the hero and the chief comic character one and the same person. (Not even inverted commas round the word can make Menteith the hero.) It is this identification that gives to the novel its forceful narrative sweep. Dalgetty rides alone into the story; and at the end, when all the values that have been evoked for us by our sight of the Royalists, and 'placed' for us by Dalgetty, are destroyed, he rides alone out of the story unchanged, unchangeable, except for the knighthood conferred on him for purely practical reasons by Montrose. If Dalgetty's knighthood is a piece of cynicism his sense of Honour is the most admirable we have seen in the book, and the story ends with an illustration of it. Dalgetty is taken prisoner at Philiphaugh and seems likely to die:

> Several Lowland officers, in the service of the Covenanters, interceded for Dalgetty on this occasion, representing him as a person whose skill would be useful in their army, and who

would be readily induced to change his service. But on this point they found Sir Dugald unexpectedly obstinate. He had engaged with the King for a certain term, and, till that was expired, his principles would not permit any shadow of changing. (ch. 23)

Luckily it was discovered that his engagement had only a fortnight to run; at the end of that time he changed sides and 'entered the service of the Estates'.

Dalgetty's escape from the losing side follows the pattern of other Scott heroes – Edward Waverley, Darsie Latimer, Henry Morton – and parodies and mocks Menteith's escape. Menteith (conveniently) 'did not recover sufficiently to join Montrose' and marries the daughter of one of his opponents. Dugald Dalgetty, we read, entered into 'possession of his paternal estate of Drumthwacket, which he acquired, not by the sword, but by a pacific intermarriage with Hannah Strachan, a matron somewhat stricken in years, the widow of the Aberdeenshire Covenanter'.

II

'But I maun hear naething about honour – we ken naething here but about credit.' (*Rob Roy*)

Rob Roy is not a complete success. It begins very well, but proceeds by fits and starts, and in spite of some memorable scenes and characters is often confused and confusing. Various faults have been pointed out. There is the casual, convenient killing of the Osbaldistone brothers in order that Frank may inherit their estates; there is the mystery of Mr Osbaldistone's financial troubles (how did Rashleigh have it in his power to ruin the firm of Osbaldistone and Tresham?); and there is the general aimlessness of Frank's movements in Scotland. But if the book is more clumsy and less effective than at the start it promises to be, this is not only, or mainly, because of carelessness in the details of the plot.

There is no one focus for Scott's examination of the old and new orders. At first Osbaldistone Hall is offered as the contrast to the commercial life of Frank's father:

> The abode of my fathers, which I was now approaching, was situated in a glen, or narrow valley, which ran up among those hills. Extensive estates, which once belonged to the family of Osbaldistone, had been long dissipated by the misfortunes or misconduct of my ancestors; but enough was still attached to the old mansion, to give my uncle the title of a man of large property. This he employed (as I was given to understand by some inquiries which I made on the road) in maintaining the prodigal hospitality of a northern squire of the period, which he deemed essential to the family dignity.
>
> From the summit of an eminence I had already had a distant view of Osbaldistone Hall, a large and antiquated edifice, peeping out from a Druidical grove of huge oaks, and I was directing my course towards it, as straightly and as speedily as the windings of a very indifferent road would permit, when my horse, tired as he was, pricked up his ears at the enlivening notes of a pack of hounds in full cry, cheered by the occasional bursts of a French horn, which in those days was a constant accompaniment to the chase. (ch. 5)

'Druidical' stresses not only the age of the Hall and of the way of life that is followed there, but also Frank's romantic outlook and willingness to be bewitched. This readiness to romanticise (Scott shows) comes, as with Edward Waverley, from Frank's upbringing:

> After the death of my mother, the care of nursing me during my childish illnesses, and of rendering all those tender attentions which infancy exacts from female affection, devolved on old Mabel. Interdicted by her master from speaking to him on the subject of the heaths, glades, and dales of her beloved Northumberland, she poured herself forth to my infant ear in descriptions of the scenes of her youth, and long narratives of the

events which tradition declared to have passed amongst them. To these I inclined my ear much more seriously than to graver, but less animated instructors. (ch. 4)

The willingness to be bewitched issues in Frank's flirtation with Die Vernon, as Edward Waverley's romantic attachment to the old and glamorous is symbolised by his flirtation with Flora Mac-Ivor. The contrast between Frank's father and his relations at Osbaldistone Hall shows Scott at his best. Mr Osbaldistone is, of course, very different from his relations at the Hall; he had early left the ancestral home and had early abandoned the old family faith. But just as Joshua Geddes is shown to resemble Redgauntlet and to have had ancestors who behaved as Redgauntlet behaves, so Scott tells us that Mr Osbaldistone merely directed the family temperament and instincts into other channels:

> Love of his profession was the motive which he chose should be most ostensible, when he urged me to tread the same path; but he had others with which I only became acquainted at a later period. Impetuous in his schemes, as well as skilful and daring, each new adventure, when successful, became at once the incentive, and furnished the means, for farther speculation. It seemed to be necessary to him, as to an ambitious conqueror, to push on from achievement to achievement, without stopping to secure, far less to enjoy, the acquisitions which he made. Accustomed to see his whole fortune trembling in the scales of chance, and dexterous at adopting expedients for casting the balance in his favour, his health and spirits and activity seemed ever to increase with the animating hazards on which he staked his wealth; and he resembled a sailor, accustomed to brave the billows and the foe, whose confidence rises on the eve of tempest or of battle. (ch. 1)

The language of military adventure links him with Osbaldistone Hall and the Jacobite rising of 1715. Professor Davie comments on this:

Scott insists repeatedly that old Osbaldistone is a Romantic, he is in trade, not for what he can get out of it, but for the devil of it. He likes taking commercial risks. This, which can be regarded as Scott's interpretation of Addison's figure, Sir Andrew Freeport, is a genuine contribution to the understanding of history, to the drawing of a distinction between capitalism in its first expansive and adventurous phase, and the capitalism of a later age that is above all prudent and cautious.[4]

But if Osbaldistone Hall seems at first to be Scott's picture of an older way of life, the novel soon shows us another in Rob Roy and his wife and the events of the '15. In this part of the story Mr Osbaldistone, and what he stands for, is succeeded by Bailie Nicol Jarvie. Like Frank's father the Bailie has relations who belong to a different and older world (Rob Roy and his wife); and, as with Frank's father, commercial life has not diminished the Bailie's adventurous spirit and courage. It is he supremely who draws our attention to the growth of the new commercial Scotland and to the inevitable anachronism of Rob Roy and all he represents. Like Frank's father the Bailie has little time for poetry; for him poetry and Jacobitism are idle and even mischievous day-dreams:

> Will *Tityre tu patulae*, as they ca' it, tell him where Rashleigh Osbaldistone is? or Macbeth, and all his kernes and galla-glasses, and your awn to boot, Rob, procure him five thousand pounds to answer the bills which fall due ten days hence, were they a' rouped at the Cross, basket-hilts, Andra-Ferraras, leather targets, brogues, brochan and sporrans?' (ch. 23)

Jarvie and Mr Osbaldistone represent Credit rather than Honour; both in fact insist that Credit *is* Honour – as Steenie Steenson's Honour in *Redgauntlet* consisted in securing his credit:

> 'Upon all these matters I am now to ask your advice, Mr Jarvie, which, I have no doubt, will point out the best way to act for my father's advantage and my own honour.'

'Ye're right, young man – ye're right', said the Bailie. 'Aye take the counsel of those who are aulder and wiser than your-sell . . . But I maun hear naething about honour – we ken naithing here but about credit. Honour is a homicide and a bloodspiller, that gangs about making frays in the street; but Credit is a decent honest man, that sits at hame, and makes the pat play.' (ch. 26)

The contrast between Honour and Credit, between old and new, is developed in many ways. Frank admits to Die Vernon his ignorance of heraldry:

'You an Osbaldistone, and confess so much!' she exclaimed. 'Why, Percie, Thornie, John Dickson – Wilfred himself, might be your instructor – Even ignorance itself is a plummet over you.'

'With shame I confess it, my dear Miss Vernon, the mys-teries couched under the grim hieroglyphics of heraldry are to me as unintelligible as those of the Pyramids of Egypt.'

'What! is it possible? – Why, even my uncle reads Gwillym sometimes of a winter night – Not know the figures of heraldry? – of what could your father be thinking?'

'Of the figures of arithmetic,' I answered; 'the most insignifi-cant unit of which he holds more highly than all the blazonry of chivalry.' (ch. 10)

And if Die Vernon is allowed to ask – 'Then in the name of Heaven, Mr Francis Osbaldistone, what *can* you do?' – it is Scott's way of ensuring that our respect will be for his father, or Rob Roy, or the Bailie, but not for Frank.

If *Rob Roy* lacks the narrative thrust and coherence of *Waverley* or *The Legend of Montrose*, the narrative clumsi-ness and shift of focus are not alone to blame. For many critics it is the two chief comic characters, Bailie Nicol Jarvie and Andrew Fairservice, who are responsible for the novel's failure. The objections to these two always take the same form. Professor Davie writes:

Yet it could be maintained that in him [Jarvie] we have the most elaborate piece of full-length 'realistic' presentation in the whole work. This is certainly true. But it is also true that Jarvie bursts out of his frame; and whereas some critics seem to take this as the highest praise, I mean by it rather to deplore once again Scott's slipshod method, his lack of concern for the internal economy of his composition. Scott's presentation of Jarvie is 'realistic' as some of Dicken's presentations are realistic; he belongs in some unwritten novel as loose, exuberant and intricate as *Martin Chuzzlewit*.[5]

His comments on Fairservice are even sharper:

We are sometimes asked to applaud the vitality of the figures of Jarvie and Andrew Fairservice, and to contrast this with the woodenness of the villain, Rashleigh, of the heroine, Diana Vernon, and indeed of the hero, Frank. But this, is to beg an important question. Vitality, yes – but to what purpose? The trouble with Nicol Jarvie is that this figure has altogether too much vitality for the good of the book as a whole. And if this is true of Jarvie, it is still more true of Fairservice, who is nothing more than one huge excrescence on the story. He has no part to play in the logic of the theme, so far as this can be discerned.[6]

We cannot defend Scott by saying that the characters are delightful. If in other novels Scott can create comic characters who are also essential to the book's narrative structure, we cannot then say of *Rob Roy* that this is to ask too much of him.

Scott's intention with Fairservice is plain, but the intention is not fully realised. Fairservice is to parody and thus to 'place' the hero (Frank), just as Peter Peebles parodies Redgauntlet, and as Dugald Dalgetty parodies, in his entanglement with and escape from an older, more glamorous way of life, the usual Scott hero. In *Rob Roy*, Francis Osbaldistone is the familiar peripatetic hero. On the first part of his travels, from London to Osbaldistone Hall, he is alone; but when he leaves Northumberland for

Scotland, Andrew Fairservice goes with him. They leave together, these two Protestants, neither of whom belongs to Northumberland. They are both cautious and have both the same terrified reaction to Scotland. And they both survive. If it is clever of Frank to evade so neatly the consequences of his entanglement with Rob Roy and the Jacobites, and to inherit the ancestral home, it is a cleverness that Scott mocks through the conclusion to Andrew Fairservice's own adventures. Frank describes the fight at Osbaldistone Hall when Rashleigh is killed and Die Vernon and her father are rescued by Rob Roy:

> I now resolved to go myself, but in my way I stumbled over the body of a man, as I thought, dead or dying. It was, however, Andrew Fairservice, as well and whole as ever he was in his life, who had only taken this recumbent posture to avoid the slashes, stabs, and pistol-balls, which, for a moment or two, were flying in various directions.

The scene affects us in the same way as Falstaff's inglorious survival. Scott is the only writer of the romantic period who was influenced by Shakespeare without being overwhelmed by him, and who could make his borrowings from Shakespeare a vital part of his own work. (Another obvious example is the three 'cummers' in *The Bride of Lammermoor*.) Perhaps the explanation is that Scott's major work is in prose.

Bailie Nicol Jarvie is in many ways a parallel to Frank's father. But again with him, as with Fairservice, we can see how Scott intended that his comic characters should carry the weight of the book. In the scene at the clachan of Aberfoil the Bailie takes on symbolic force – this is why the scene is so well known. When he attacks the 'gigantic Highlander' with a firebrand so successfully that his enemy is forced to retreat, he acts out the essential shape of all these Scott novels which tell of the inevitable defeat of an older way of life by the new commercial Scotland.

Professor Davie writes:

> In Scotland when Scott wrote no question was so vital as that of the possibility of 'marrying' two cultural traditions – the one barbarous and heroic, the other Hanoverian. When Waverley chooses to marry Rose Bradwardine he acts out Scott's answer to this question. The relations between Frank Osbaldistone and Diana Vernon continually promise some such symbolic meaning, but the promise is never redeemed.[7]

Scott's answer is that no such marrying is posisble. (In his own life the only attempt at a solution was to build Abbotsford and fill it with antiquarian bric-a-brac.) Much of the strength and worth of the novels comes from this same recognition that the 'barbarous and heroic' and the 'Hanoverian' cannot marry. Professor Davie is wrong to see Rose Bradwardine as the equivalent of Diana Vernon; it is Flora Mac-Ivor who is the true parallel. Rose Bradwardine has 'sat still while kings are arming'. The failure of Edward and Flora to marry in *Waverley* is certainly symbolic; but I am not sure that the 'promise of some such symbolic meaning' is, in the relations between Frank Osbaldistone and Diana Vernon, 'never redeemed'. Scott makes the mistake (artistic and historical: the two cannot be separated) of letting them marry, though every reader knows that this is wrong. Scott knew, too, that this was wrong and tried to combine a 'happy ending' with what he knew to be the truth about this older way of life (Die Vernon) with which Frank has flirted. Professor Welsh makes the point well:

> As it is, critics have traditionally sensed that the hero and heroine should have parted forever in the Highlands. Scott himself seems to have felt the force of his exception, for he qualifies the denouement of *Rob Roy* in an interesting fashion. On the last

AW D

page of the romance the reader suddenly learns that Die Vernon is dead when these memoirs are being written. She is last spoken of as 'lamented': 'You know how long I lamented her; but you do not know – cannot know, how much she deserved her husband's sorrow.' This is all very much in the past tense; there is no suggestion that any children are born to them; there is none of the sense of futurity which a proper hero and heroine ought to enjoy. With the intuitive sense of poetic justice shared by his critics, Scott makes death the last word for Die.[8]

5 'The Bride of Lammermoor'

'. . . why, old man, would you cling to a falling tower?'
(*The Bride of Lammermoor*)

. . . the very conception and main structure of his stories is in some instances purely poetical. Take as an example the *Bride of Lammermoor*. Through the progress of that deeply affecting tale, from the gloomy and agitating scene of Lord Ravenswood's funeral to the final agony and appalling death of his ill-fated heir, we experience that fervour and exaltation of mind, that keen susceptibility of emotion, and that towering and perturbed state of the imagination, which poetry alone can produce. Thus, while the events are comparatively few, and the whole plan and conduct of the tale unusually simple, our passions are fully exercised and our expectations even painfully excited, by occurrences in themselves unimportant, conversations without any material result, and descriptions which retard the main action. The principal character is strikingly poetical, and its effect skilfully heightened by the manner in which the subordinate figures, even those of a grotesque outline, are grouped around it.[1]

I T is usual to refer to *The Bride of Lammermoor* as a special case and to point to what distinguishes it from Scott's other novels. Lockhart tells of the physical agony that Scott suffered as he dictated the book to his amanuenses, and in a well-known passage recounts how Scott read the novel when it was published but 'did not recollect one single incident, character or conversation it contained'![2] We come to the novel expecting it to be different, and the differences are what we notice first. Ravenswood does not seem to be the usual Scott hero. The passivity that normally marks Scott's young men is here transferred to the heroine, Lucy, and the account of her disposition and gentle undisciplined Fancy in chapter 3 makes her seem like Waverley's sister. Ravenswood is Vich Ian Vohr, not Waverley; more aptly, perhaps, he is Redgauntlet and neither Darsie Latimer nor Alan Fairford. The novel, indeed, is nearer to *Redgauntlet* than to any other. Ravenswood, like Redgauntlet, is mad; his gloomy disposition is stressed; his various actions are those of someone unbalanced, and at the end of the book the point is made clear. We see there his paroxysms of uncontrolled mental agony and we learn that his death in the Kelpie's Flow is suicide:

> 'Oh, sir! oh master! kill me if you will, but do not go out on this dreadful errand! Oh! My dear master, wait but this day – The Marquis of A—— comes to-morrow, and a' will be remedied.'
>   'You have no longer a master, Caleb', said Ravenswood, endeavouring to extricate himself; 'why, old man, would you cling to a falling tower?' . . . 'Caleb!' he said with a ghastly smile, 'I make you my executor.' (ch. 35)

The 'dreadful errand' is the duel with Lucy Ashton's brother. Ravenswood hopes he will be there; he does not ride through the quick-sands deliberately. We are scarcely invited to sympathise with Ravenswood; Scott does not see him as a Romantic or Byronic hero. He is mad in the same way and for the same reasons that Redgauntlet is mad.

Ravenswood is unlike the usual Scott hero in other ways; he does not wander (as do Henry Morton, Edward Waverley, Darsie Latimer and Francis Osbaldistone); he is not (as they are) the means of contrasting two different cultures and of holding their attractions momentarily in balance. The point of the book is that Ravenswood cannot wander, that he cannot move away from the 'falling tower'. He is not interested in politics, although the decline in the family fortunes is owing, at least in part, to political change: the hero's apartness and lack of public concern make *The Bride of Lammermoor* seem at first less of an historical novel than *Redgauntlet*. Ravenswood's failure to adapt himself to change relates only to his character or psychology and not to the presence of any other valuable and older way of life that might make such change not totally attractive. Ravenswood's failure is a personal one; Redgauntlet's failure is the failure of something larger and is more poignant. 'Scott's greatness', writes Lukács, 'lies in his capacity to give living human embodiment to historical-social types.'[3] Again, this is less true of *The Bride of Lammermoor*; the only important exception in that novel is Caleb Balderstone, and it is interesting that much of the success of the book can be attributed to him.

These differences are interesting but less important than those things which *The Bride of Lammermoor* has in common with Scott's other novels; Scott's narrative method remains the same. Adolphus has recorded above his enthusiasm for the novel and has noted the simplicity of the tale, but his shrewd comments are misleading in two ways. He gives no idea of the comedy in the novel and misunderstands Scott's narrative method by referring to a number of incidents 'which, although rather appendages than essential parts of the principal narrative, in fact constitute its chief beauty as a work of imagination'.[4] Again, Adolphus writes: 'I treat these as appendages, because the story might be told without them; but everyone must feel that without them the story would not be worth telling.'[5] This is an early statement of what has been too general a way of considering Scott's novels: there is something in Scott's novels called a story, which is probably not worth telling, but is enlivened from time to time by incidents or scenes or characters – mere appendages – which make the novel worth reading. Adolphus, like others, goes wrong because he is not true to his own reaction to the novel. How could he, or we, experience 'through the whole progress of that deeply affecting tale' that 'fervour and exaltation of mind' if the things in the novel which keeps us in this 'towering and perturbed state of the imagination' were simply appendages to an abstraction called 'story'? It is not that 'without them the story would not be worth telling', but that without them there would be no 'story' to tell. Adolphus fails to analyse his sensitive response to Scott because he uses the wrong critical tools.

The novel is another description by Scott of failure to change with the changing times. Ravenswood's is the obvious failure in the novel, but not the only one; for Caleb Balderstone parodies his master in this, and cannot admit that times have changed, and, for most people, changed for the better. The cost of this failure in Scott's novels is always high. It is sometimes death from despair, from a refusal to go on living when the older ways of life are destroyed, as with Caleb Balderstone; it can lead to a total withdrawal from the world, as with Flora Mac-Ivor; it can lead to madness, as with Redgauntlet and Ravenswood.

On the first page of the novel, in chapter 2,[6] we learn of the decline in the fortunes of the Ravenswood family. The hero's father had espoused the 'sinking side' in the civil war of 1689; his title had been abolished in consequence, but the decline in the family fortunes is not traced to any political or social cause ('their house had its revolutions like all sublunary things. It became greatly declined from its splendour about the middle of the seventeenth century . . .') although he blames (possibly unjustly) the final fall in his fortunes on a political opponent. Certainly he is 'far from bending his mind to his new condition of life', and at his funeral – it is the opening scene of the novel – his son, the Master of Ravenswood, shows that he has inherited the same prejudices, the same wish to place the blame for the ruined family fortunes on Sir William Ashton and to swear revenge on him and his family. The scene is important and impressively tells us what the novel is about. It is not only the hero's father who is buried: 'Under the very arch of the house of death, the clergyman, affrighted at the scene, and trembling for his own safety, hastily and unwillingly rehearsed the solemn service of the church, and spoke dust to dust, and ashes to ashes, over ruined pride and decayed prosperity' (ch. 2). The Master of Ravenswood, like his father, is 'far from bending his mind to his new condition of life'; and the more he sees that the former family prosperity and greatness are dead and buried, the more he clings obsessively to fantastic and chimerical notions of Honour. As in *Redgauntlet* and *Waverley*, Scott gives these notions of Honour to those who cannot move with the times and accept inevitable change. Baron Bradwardine had said when his fortunes had crashed that 'a house has stood lang eneugh if it stands till it falls with honour', and this flexibility and good sense earn him Scott's approval; but the 'Honour' of Ravenswood is the 'Honour' of Redgauntlet and Vich Ian Vohr. If we sympathise less with Ravenswood than with these others, it is because they are concerned for a political cause. Ravenswood's thoughts in the first chapter turn more selfishly on 'the tarnished honour and degraded fortunes of his house, the destruction of his own hopes, and the triumph of that family by whom they had been ruined'.

In chapter 4 we meet Blind Alice – one of the 'mere appendages' to the book – and through her the question of accepting inevitable change is raised again. Sir William Ashton and Lucy go to visit her:

'You have been long a resident on this property?' he said, after a pause.

'It is now nearly sixty years since I first knew Ravenswood,' answered the old dame . . .

'You are not, I should judge by your accent, of the country originally?' said the Lord Keeper, in continuation.

'No; I am by birth an Englishwoman.'

'Yet you seem attached to this country, as if it were your own.'

'It is here,' replied the blind woman, 'that I have drunk the cup of joy and sorrow which Heaven destined for me. I was here the wife of an upright and affectionate husband for more than twenty years; I was here the mother of six promising children; it was here that God deprived me of all these blessings; it was here they died, and yonder, by yon ruined chapel, they lie all buried. I had no country but theirs while they lived; I have none but theirs now they are no more.'

'But your house,' said the Lord Keeper, looking at it, 'is miserably ruinous?'

'Do, my dear father,' said Lucy, eagerly, yet bashfully, catching at the hint, 'give orders to make it better – that is, if you think it proper.'

'It will last my time, my dear Miss Lucy,' said the blind woman; 'I would not have my lord give himself the least trouble about it.'

'But,' said Lucy, 'you once had a much better house and were rich; and now in your old age to live in this hovel!'

'It is as good as I deserve, Miss Lucy. If my heart has not broke with what I have suffered, and seen others suffer, it must have been strong enough; and the rest of this old frame has no right to call itself weaker.'

'You have probably witnessed many changes,' said the Lord

Keeper; 'but your experience must have taught you to expect
them.'

'It has taught me to endure them, my lord,' was the reply.

'Yet you knew that they must needs arrive in the course of
years?' said the statesman.

'Ay, as I know that the stump, on or beside which you sit,
once a tall and lofty tree, must needs one day fall by decay or
by the axe; yet I hoped my eyes might not witness the downfall
of the tree which overshadowed my dwelling.'

The passage is central to the novel. Like Ravenswood,
Blind Alice has lost all her family; like him she has a
house which is 'miserably ruinous'; like him she 'once had
a much better house, and was rich'; unlike him she has
learnt to endure change. In the last words of the passage
the reference to the tree which overshadowed her dwelling
(symbolic of the house[7] of Ravenswood, which formerly
gave her protection) connects her experience, and her
reaction to it, with Ravenswood's. The opening chapters,
then, show us two different ways of reacting to inevitable
change; and the whole novel is shaped to comment on
Ravenswood's behaviour and on the trivial notions of
honour that dictate it.

Because in the novel Scott introduces the supernatural
and uses the three old 'cummers' as a chorus, it is sometimes thought of as a novel of Fate, a tragedy of Chance.
Ravenswood looks upon the events of his life in this way
('There is ill luck, I think, in whatever belongs to me'),
but in fact he is responsible for what happens to him and
his house. Scott's central interest in the best of his Scottish novels is the response of the individual to changing
social and economic conditions. Even in *The Bride of
Lammermoor* he is first of all an historical novelist. There
is no need to trace how the various details of the novel
contribute to the total shape and have their significance

determined by that shape, but it is worth while considering the part played (as in the other novels) by the comic
character (in this book there is only one) in the total
structure.

We first meet Caleb Balderstone in chapter 7, when
Ravenswood returns to the tower of Wolf's Crag with –
for Caleb that most unwelcome of accompaniments – a
guest. After delaying their entry as long as possible,

'Is it you, my dear master? is it you yourself, indeed?' exclaimed
the old domestic. 'I am wae ye suld hae stude waiting at your ain
gate; but wha wad hae thought o' seeing ye sae sune, and a
strange gentleman with a' – (Here he exclaimed apart, as it were,
and to some inmate of the tower, in a voice not meant to be
heard by those in the court, 'Mysie – Mysie woman! stir for dear
life, and get the fire mended; take the auld three-legged stool, or
onything that's readiest that will make a lowe.') – 'I doubt we
are but puirly provided, no expecting ye this some months, when
doubtless ye wad hae been received conform till your rank, as
gude right is; but natheless –'

'Natheless, Caleb,' said the Master, 'we must have our horses
put up, and ourselves too, the best way we can. I hope you are
not sorry to see me sooner than you expected?'

'Sorry, my lord! I am sure ye sall aye be my lord wi' honest
folk, as your noble ancestors hae been these three hundred
years, and never asked a Whig's leave. Sorry to see the Lord of
Ravenswood at ane o' his ain castles!' – (Then again apart to his
unseen associate behind the screen, 'Mysie, kill the brood-hen
without thinking twice on it; let them care that come ahint.') –
'No to say it's our best dwelling,' he added, turning to Bucklaw;
'but just a strength for the Lord of Ravenswood to flee until –
that is, no to *flee*, but to retreat until in troublous times, like the
present, when it was ill convenient for him to live farther in the
country in ony of his better and mair principal manors; but, for
its antiquity, maist folk think that the outside of Wolf's Crag is
worthy of a large perusal.'

'And you are determined we shall have time to make it,' said

Ravenswood, somewhat amused with the shifts the old man used to detain them without doors, until his confederate Mysie had made her preparations within.

'Oh, never mind the outside of the house, my good friend,' said Bucklaw; 'let's see the inside, and let our horses see the stable, that's all.'

'Oh, yes, sir – ay, sir – unquestionably, sir – my lord and ony of his honourable companions –'

'But our horses, my old friend – our horses; they will be dead-foundered by standing here in the cold after riding hard, and mine is too good to be spoiled; therefore, once more, our horses,' exclaimed Bucklaw.

'True – ay – your horses – yes – I will call the grooms;' and sturdily did Caleb roar till the old tower rang again. 'John – William – Saunders! – The lads are gane out, or sleeping,' he observed, after pausing for an answer, which he knew that he had no human chance of receiving. A' gaes wrang when the Master's out by; but I'll take care o' your cattle mysell.'

'I think you had better,' said Ravenswood, 'otherwise I see little chance of their being attended to at all.'

'Whisht, my lord – whisht, for God's sake,' said Caleb in an imploring tone, and apart to his master; 'if ye dinna regard your ain credit, think on mine; we'll hae hard eneugh wark to mak a decent nigh o't a' the less I can tell.'

This first scene with Caleb establishes the main points of his character; there is his zeal for what he believes to be the Honour of the house of Ravenswood, his resource in concealing (or attempting to conceal) the straitened circumstances of the family, and his inability to recognise that times have changed and (whatever the fortunes of his master's family may be) for most people have changed for the better. Caleb parodies, and thus 'places', Ravenswood's fierce attachment to what he, too, considers family Honour, and his suicidal inability to adapt himself to new times and new conditions. Caleb is Scott's comment on Ravenswood, just as Peter Peebles is one of his comments on Redgauntlet.[8] *The Bride of Lammermoor* is no less an historical novel than *Waverley* or *Redgauntlet*, for it shows here, to quote Lukács, 'how important historical changes affect everyday life'.[9]

How treacherous some notions of honour can be, and how corrupting the wish to 'call back yesterday, bid time return' is often comically plain in the adventures of Caleb. He wonders how to get provisions in the village without paying for them:

> 'There's Eppie Sma'trash will trust us for all,' said Caleb to himself; 'she has lived a' her life under the family – and maybe wi' a soup brandy – I canna say for wine – she is but a lone woman, and gets her claret by a runlet at a time – but I'll work a wee drap out o' her by fair means or foul. For doos, there's the doocot; there will be poultry amang the tenants, though Luckie Chirnside says she has paid the kain twice ower. We'll mak shift, an it like your honour – we'll mak shift – keep your keart abune, for the house sall haud its credit as lang as auld Caleb is to the fore.' (ch. 8)

The determination in the closing words to uphold the Credit of the house is the same as Ravenswood's concern for its Honour, and we note that for Caleb the Credit of the house is consistent with getting wine from Eppie Sma'trash 'by fair means or foul'. For Professor Welsh 'irony seems foreign to Scott's mind'; but the structure of *The Bride of Lammermoor*, with the eccentricities and comedy of Caleb acting as a constant criticism of Ravenswood, is wholly ironic. And it is this irony and not the simple irony of Lucy Ashton's song, or any irony of fulfilled prophesy, that gives the novel its distinctive shape.

The foolishness of Caleb's concerns is made clearer by the fact that for the people of the neighbourhood, the inhabitants of the village of Wolf's-hope, the changing times have brought nothing but gain. They continued to

pay 'a kind of hereditary respect to the Lords of Ravenswood', but recently, because of the difficulties of the
Ravenswood family, 'most of the inhabitants of Wolf's-
hope had contrived to get feu-rights to their little posses-
sions . . . so that they were emancipated from the claims of
feudal dependence'. All this is galling to Caleb, 'who had
been wont to exercise over them the same sweeping
authority in levying contributions which was exercised in
former times in England', and Caleb 'loved the memory
and resented the downfall of that authority'. Caleb
attempts to exact produce for Ravenswood by referring
to custom and former usage, but all these claims are
defeated by the lawyer, Davie Dingwall, employed by the
villagers for the very purpose of confirming their complete freedom from all such attempted exactions, or, in
Caleb's phrase, 'that due and fitting connection between
superior and vassal'. When Caleb hints that his master
may use violence to enforce his claims, the lawyer answers
that his clients

'had determined to do the best they could for their own town,
and he thought Lord Ravenswood, since he was a lord, might
have enough to do to look after his own castle. As to any threats
of stouthrief oppression, by rule of thumb or *via facti*, as the law
termed it, he would have Mr Balderstone recollect that new
times were not as old times – that they lived in the south of the
Forth, and far from the Highlands – that his clients thought they
were able to protect themselves; but should they find themselves
mistaken they would apply to the government for the protection
of a corporal and four red-coats, who,' said Mr Dingwall with
a grin, 'would be perfectly able to secure them against Lord
Ravenswood, and all that he or his followers could do by the
strong hand.' (ch. 12)

(Joshua Geddes rejected Redgauntlet's appeal to custom
and former usage over the question of salmon-fishing,

and, when threatened, called the law and the red-coats to his aid.) The houses in the village offer a prosperous appearance, in vivid contrast to the dreariness of life at Wolf's Crag; the villagers are enjoying a prosperity they have not had before, and this contrast is made vivid for us in the comic scene where Caleb steals the fowl from the spit in the cooper's kitchen. The scene is a comment on Caleb's concern for the Honour of the Ravenswood family, and the word 'Honour' is shown to be a nothing-meaning term, just as we see it is for Ravenswood himself.

There is no need to look in further detail at Caleb's function in the novel. It will be enough to notice that Caleb, like Ravenswood, dies at the end of the book. Like Ravenswood he dies because he does not want to live; and like Ravenswood he does not want to live because the world has changed too much for him and he cannot face the present. 'His whole course of ideas . . . had all arisen from his close connection with the family which was now extinguished.' In the structure of the novel he has a 'close connection' of another sort with Ravenswood. As with the comic characters in *Rob Roy* and *Redgauntlet* he is Scott's way of directing our judgement on the central figure in the novel.

If a simple pining away is Caleb's fate, madness is Ravenswood's. In chapter I8 Caleb reminds his master of the prophecy:

'When the last Laird of Ravenswood to Ravenswood shall ride,
  And woo a dead maiden to be his bride,
  He shall stable his steed in the Kelpie's flow,
  And his name shall be lost for evermoe!'

  'I know the Kelpie's flow well enough,' said the Master – 'I suppose, at least, you mean the quicksand betwixt this tower and Wolf's-hope – but why any man in his senses should stable a steed there –'

But Ravenswood is not in his senses when, at the end, he rides his horse over the treacherous sands.

To mention the prophecy is to recall that aspect of the story — the use of the supernatural — which has always seemed to distinguish it most sharply from other of Scott's novels and to give it a different shape — the shape of Greek tragedy, as some critics have suggested. But Scott's use of the supernatural is not simple. Sometimes he suggests that the novel is a tale of prophecy fulfilled. In chapter 17 we read that 'the real charms of the daughter, joined to the supposed services of the father, cancelled in his memory the vows of vengeance which he had taken so deeply on the eve of his father's funeral. But they had been heard and registered in the book of fate', but normally the action of the book runs against any supernatural interpretation. Scott's chief interest lies in showing that Ravenswood's death results from personal failure and cannot be blamed on fate. And this supports a remark by Lukács: 'the historical subject-matter of his novels is very close to that of the Romantics proper . . . Scott's interpretation of this subject-matter is entirely opposed to that of the Romantics, as is his manner of portrayal.'[10] The legend of the fountain is inserted in the novel (chapter 5). Scott hedges and takes refuge in his role of editor when he tells in chapter 23 of Ravenswood's glimpse of the ghost of Alice, Blind Alice's own prophetic warnings to the Lord Keeper in chapter 4 have nothing supernatural about them; they are based on her shrewd knowledge of human nature and of the Master of Ravenswood. And there is nothing at all supernatural about Mortsheugh, the sexton, or about the three old women or 'cummers'.

Chapter 24 belongs to the sexton, and the point of it is clear. As we near the end of the novel the sexton affirms that the past to which Ravenswood clings had no value for anyone else, and that the passage of time has brought only progress and improvement. He gives a deflating, realistic account of the battle of Bothwell Brig at which he was compelled to be present by the Master of Ravenswood's grandfather, and then comments toughly and acutely on the Ravenswood family:

'They are no favourites, then, of yours, these Ravenswoods?' said the Master . . .
'I kenna wha should favour them,' said the grave-digger. 'When they had lands and power, they were ill guides of them baith; and now their head's down, there's few care how lang they may be of lifting it again.'
'Indeed!' said Ravenswood; 'I never heard that this unhappy family deserved ill-will at the hands of their country. I grant their poverty – if that renders them contemptible.'
'It will gang a far way till't,' said the sexton of Hermitage, 'ye may tak my word for that – at least, I ken naething else that suld mak myself contemptible, and folk are far frae respecting me as they wad do if I lived in a twa-lofted sclated house. But as for the Ravenswoods, I hae seen three generations of them, and deil ane to mend other.' . . .
'If Lord Ravenswood protected his people, my friend, while he had the means of doing so, I think they might spare his memory,' replied the Master.
'Ye are welcome to your ain opinion, sir,' said the sexton; 'but ye winna persuade me that he did his duty, either to himsell or to huz puir dependent cretures, in guiding us the gate he has done. He might hae gien us different tacks of our bits o' houses and yards – and me, that's an auld man, living in yonder miserable cabin, that's fitter for the dead than the quick, and killed wi' rheumatise, and John Smith in my dainty bit mailing, and his window glazen, and a' because Ravenswood guided his gear like a fule!'

The effect of this is to make more trivial still the 'Honour' that is Ravenswood's concern; and the note is struck again with a wider, fiercer reference in the words of the three 'cummers' who come to prepare the body of Blind Alice, and later to attend the marriage of Lucy and Bucklaw:

'Johnny Mortsheugh,' said Annie Winnie, 'might hae minded auld lang syne, and thought of his auld kimmers, for as braw as he is with his new black coat. I hae gotten but five herrings instead o' sax; and this disna look like a gude saxpennys; and I daresay this bit morsel o' beef is an unce lighter than ony that's been dealt round; and its a bit of the tenony hough, mair by token that yours, Maggie, is out o' the back sey'.

'Mine, quo' she?' mumbled the paralytic hag; 'mine is half banes, I trow. If grit folks gie poor bodies onthing for coming to their weddings and burials, it suld be something that wad do them gude, I think.'

'Their gifts,' said Ailsie Gourlay, 'are dealt for nae love of us — nor out of respect for whether we feed or starve. They wad gie us whinstanes for loaves, if it would serve their ain vanity; and yet they expect us to be grateful', as they ca' it, as if they served us for true love and liking.'

'And that's truly said,' answered her companion.

'But, Ailsie Gourlay, ye're the auldest o' us three — did ye ever see a mair grand bridal?'

'I winna say that I have,' answered the hag; 'but I think soon to see as braw a burial.'

'And that wad please me as weel,' said Annie Winnie; 'for there's as large a dole, and folk are no obliged to girn and laugh, and mak murgeons, and wish joy to these hellicat quality, that lord it ower us like brute beasts.' (ch. 34)

This sane, savage, ironic, levelling condemnation of the high and the mighty is the final word in the book on Ravenswood and his concept of Honour. There is no denying what they say; they speak with authority (the authority of the whole novel), and Scott, once again, has used these 'mere appendages' to shape and comment on the action.

6 'Redgauntlet'

'. . . the cause is lost for ever!' (*Redgauntlet*)

Redgauntlet and *Waverley* are Scott's most successful attempts to define his feelings towards the old Scotland and the new. Scott is often praised for his skill in character creation, and especially for the creation of comic characters. In *Redgauntlet* he has subdued this gift to a single dramatic intention, and has used his comic characters as the means by which that intention is achieved. This dramatic aim may, very briefly, be described as the attempt to answer the question: 'What qualities of mind and character are necessary to reconcile a deep love of the past with successful living in the present?' It is a great historical novel because Scott tackles with art and energy this urgent question which lies at the heart of all the Waverley novels, and because this urgency is concerned not only with the rapid social and economic changes of post-Culloden Scotland (Scott writes historical, not social, novels), but with the central and perennial question of man's relationship with the past and the present, and the need and cost of movement, change and survival.

Scott's interest is well known. In the 'Postscript, which should have been a Preface' to *Waverley* he writes:

There is no European nation, which, within the course of half a century, or little more, has undergone so complete a change as this kingdom of Scotland. The effects of the Insurrection of 1745, — the destruction of the patriarchal power of the Highland chiefs, — the abolition of the heritable jurisdictions of the

Lowland nobility and barons, – the total eradication of the Jacobite party, which, averse to intermingle with the English, or adopt their customs, long continued to pride themselves upon maintaining ancient Scottish manners and customs, – commenced this innovation. The gradual influx of wealth, and extension of commerce, have since united to render the present people of Scotland a class of beings as different from their grandfathers, as the existing English are from those of Queen Elizabeth's time ... But the change, though steadily and rapidly progressive, has, nevertheless, been gradual; and, like those who drift down the stream of a deep and smooth river, we are not aware of the progress we have made until we fix our eye on the now distant point from which we have been drifted. Such of the present generation as can recollect the last twenty or twenty-five years of the eighteenth century, will be fully sensible of the truth of this statement; especially if their acquaintance and connections lay among those who, in my younger time, were facetiously called 'folks of the old leaven', who still cherished a lingering, though hopeless attachment to the house of Stewart. This race has now almost entirely vanished from the land, and with it, doubtless, much absurd political prejudice; but also, many living examples of singular and disinterested attachment to the principles of loyalty which they received from their fathers, and of old Scottish faith, hospitality, worth, and honour.

Scott, as the final words make plain, sees Jacobitism not as a political faith, but as an older way of life, a different culture; and he recognises that it is partly 'the gradual influx of wealth, and extension of commerce' that have killed it. We sometimes speak as though this older way of life was killed on the field of Culloden and by the subsequent legal measures aimed at destroying the social system (it is not just a question of clans) that supported this former culture. (There is specific reference in *Redgauntlet* to the Act of 1748 which abolished vassalage and hereditary jurisdiction.[1]) But Scott shows that it would have died in any case. Scott's attitude to this past and to the less glamorous present is what gives pressure to all his finest Scottish novels. It is an attitude which changed between the publication of *Waverley* in 1814 and the publication of *Redgauntlet* in 1824; and the difference is related to the fact that the action of *Redgauntlet* takes place in 1763 or 1764 – eighteen years after the rising of 1745. Some of the pathos of the novel comes from our recognition (Redgauntlet does not, of course, recognise it) that in the space of these eighteen years the old order has been destroyed. In *Waverley* the great clan leader Vich Ian Vohr, otherwise Glennaquoich, is captured with his lieutenant Evan Maccombich; and at Carlisle Castle they are tried and sentenced to death. Evan rises to address the court when he hears the death-sentence passed on his master.

There was a murmur of compassion among the spectators, from the idea that the poor fellow intended to plead the influence of his superior as an excuse for his crime. The Judge commanded silence, and encouraged Evan to proceed.

'I was only ganging to say, my lord,' said Evan, in what he meant to be an insinuating manner, 'that if Your Excellent Honour, and the Honourable Court, would let Vich Ian Vohr go free just this once, and let him gae back to France, and no to trouble King George's government again, that ony six o' the very best of his clan will be willing to be justified in his stead; and if you'll just let me gae down to Glennaquoich, I'll fetch them up to ye mysell, to head or hand, and you may begin wi' me the very first man.'

Notwithstanding the solemnity of the occasion, a sort of laugh was heard in the court at the extraordinary nature of the proposal. The Judge checked this indecency, and Evan, looking sternly around, when the murmur abated, 'If the Saxon gentlemen are laughing,' he said, 'because a poor man, such as me, thinks my life, or the life of six of my degree, is worth that of Vich Ian Vohr, it's like enough they may be very right; but if they laugh because they think I would not keep my word, and come back to redeem him, I can tell them they ken neither the heart of a Hielandman, nor the honour of a gentleman.' (ch. 68)

There is no Evan Maccombich in *Redgauntlet*. The lieutenant, Cristal Nixon, betrays his master; the Misses Arthuret are loyal but fatuous, and the other conspirators in Joe Crackenthorp's public-house are chiefly anxious to save themselves. Vich Ian Vohr is beaten in battle and hanged; Redgauntlet is beaten by the passage of time and is dismissed in anti-climax. In the last scene he stands as the representative of the older Scotland, and we see him as glamorous, heroic, selfless and futile – an anachronism in 1763.

It is by means of the characters, chiefly the comic characters, that Scott defines his attitude to Redgauntlet and through him to so much else. No comic character runs away with the story, or is there for his own sake; but all are controlled by Scott's artistic purpose and serve it efficiently. The story of Peter Peebles, for example, is a comic sub-plot which controls our reaction to the total narrative; and one of the ways in which Scott builds his complex feelings towards Redgauntlet is by suggesting a parallel between him and Peter Peebles. Peter Peebles is an absurd and pathetic 'insane pauper' who has been ruined in mind, body and estate by the Law, by endless processes of litigation.

His hair, half grey, half black, escaped in elf-locks around a huge wig, made of tow, as it seemed to me, and so much shrunk that it stood upon the very top of his head; above which he plants, when covered, an immense cocked hat, which, like the chieftain's banner in an ancient battle, may be seen any sederunt day betwixt nine and ten, high towering above all the fluctuating and changeful scene in the Outer House . . . His countenance, originally that of a portly, comely burgess, is now emaciated with

poverty and anxiety, and rendered wild by an insane lightness
about the eyes. (Letter 13)

Superficially there is no resemblance to Redgauntlet.
But both of them have been ruined by the Law; and both
of them spend their time and energy obsessively trying to
resuscitate a lost and hopeless cause. (The picture of his
cocked hat 'like the chieftain's banner in an ancient battle'
helps to connect him with Redgauntlet in this respect.)
They are the two unsuccessful men in the novel, whose
unsuccess is defined as an incapacity to live in the present.
Scott draws attention to the parallel by telling us that the
lawsuit which brought disaster on Peter Peebles dates
from 1745. And he so interweaves these two characters
that in the final scene, as we shall see, the folly of Peter
Peebles makes us wonder if the heroism and gesturing of
Redgauntlet are not folly too. In the 'Conclusion' to the
novel we learn of Redgauntlet that 'as he has hinted to
General Campbell, he exchanged his residence for the
cloister'; and Scott suggests that this ending to Redgauntlet's life is similar to the 'perplexity fit' which, we
are told a few lines before, suddenly killed Peter Peebles.
Neither can live in the world as it is.

'Honour' is a word that Redgauntlet often uses; it is
'Honour' that dictates all he does, and which should, he
thinks, be the only guide in conduct. It is a part of Scott's
examination of Jacobitism to give us his own description
of Honour and to show us what kind of courage is necessary to sustain it. Once again, this description and this
demonstration are achieved by means of the characters;
but the matters are broached explicitly as well. In chapter
17 we have this: 'Those who follow the banners of
Reason are like the well-disciplined battalion, which,
wearing a more sober uniform, and making a less dazzling
show, than the light troops commanded by Imagination,

enjoy more safety, and even more honour, in the conflicts of human life.'

The implications of the military metaphor are clear. We are about to meet General Campbell with his 'well-disciplined battalion', and Redgauntlet's few reluctant followers at the end are, indeed, 'light troops'. The implied conflict in the novel between the old Scotland and the new, which Scott sees in part as a conflict between Reason and Imagination, or Reason and Romanticism, is here made explicit. And it is 'Reason' which commands the greater honour.

The question of courage is first raised in the opening letters between Darsie Latimer and Alan Fairford. Darsie has laughed at Alan Fairford, Senior's retreat at the battle of Falkirk when pursued by 'three or four mountain knaves, with naked claymores', and is rebuked by his friend:

> Imagine such a train at your own heels, Darsie, and ask your-self whether you would not exert your legs as fast as you did in flying from the Solway tide. And yet you impeach my father's courage. I tell you he has courage enough to do what is right, and to spurn what is wrong — courage enough to defend a righteous cause with hand and purse, and to take the part of the poor man against his oppressor, without fear of the consequences to himself. This is civil courage Darsie; and it is of little conse-quence to most men in this age and country whether they ever possess military courage or no. (Letter 5)

The novel demonstrates the truth of the last sentence. These opening letters in the novel are often condemned for their tedium, and it was certainly a clumsy tactic to use the epistolary method. But the letters get across to us Darsie's vapid romanticism and its remoteness from fact; and these flaws in Darsie make an oblique comment on Redgauntlet. Darsie is a tiresome young man of trivial literary interests — a feebler Waverley — whose chief characteristic is an ungoverned fancy. Alan Fairford gives him some good advice. He urges Darsie to 'view things as they are' and tells him not to look at 'ordinary events' through a 'Claud Lorraine glass'. When we meet Redgauntlet in Letter 4 he is presented as a conventional 'romantic' hero.

> He was too young, and evinced too little resignation to his fate, to resemble Belisarius. Coriolanus, standing by the hearth of Tullus Aufidius, came nearer the mark; yet the gloomy and haughty look of the stranger had, perhaps, still more of Marius seated among the ruins of Carthage.

This doesn't promise well until we remember that we are seeing Redgauntlet through the eyes of Darsie, and that Darsie has the knack of 'making histories out of nothing'. In Letter 5, when Redgauntlet under the name of Herries of Birrenswork visits the Fairford household in Edinburgh, Alan, with Darsie's lengthy description of Redgauntlet before him, does not guess that Redgauntlet and Birrenswork are the same person. This is not surprising; we do not make the connection ourselves. Seen through Alan's eyes, the eyes of common sense and reason, Redgauntlet is a very different person; and what chiefly attracts Alan's notice is his visitor's excessive use of a tooth-pick while Mr Fairford says grace.

The discussion of courage is presented in dramatic terms, and is linked with other themes of the novel, in the scene (Letter 6) where Redgauntlet meets Joshua Geddes, the Quaker, and blocks his path. 'I could not help thinking', says Darsie, 'that they might have formed no bad emblem of Peace and War.' Scott, however, is more intelligent than Darsie and sees in the Quaker much more than an 'emblem of Peace'. The courage of Geddes — moral and physical — is impressive and admired by everyone, including Redgauntlet. But, more important than this, he emerges as the representative of the new Scotland, and he is Scott's dramatisation of those social and economic changes which since 1745 have made military courage outdated and anachronistic. The quarrel between Redgauntlet and Geddes is over fishing. Redgauntlet and his friends use the older methods of line and spear. Redgauntlet (appropriately) reminds the Quaker that these are the traditional ways to fish. For Redgauntlet fishing is a sport for the gentry and a source of free food for the poorest. Geddes uses the newer methods of stake-nets, and for him fishing is a commercial undertaking. The two have quarrelled because Redgauntlet claims that the stake-nets are destroying the fishing for everyone else.

> 'I prithee' (said the Quaker) 'seek no quarrel against us, for thou shalt have no wrong at our hand.'
>
> 'Be assured I will take none at the hand of any man, whether his hat be cocked or broad-brimmed,' answered the fisherman. 'I tell you in fair terms, Joshua Geddes, that you and your partners are using unlawful craft to destroy the fish in the Solway in stake-nets and wears, and that we, who fish fairly, and like men, as our fathers did, have daily and yearly less sport and less profit. Do not think gravity or hypocrisy can carry it off as you have done. The world knows you, and we know you. You will destroy the salmon which make the livelihood of fifty poor families, and then wipe your mouth, and go to make a speech at meeting. But do not hope it will last thus. I give you fair warning, we will be upon you one morning soon, when we will not leave a stake standing in the pools of the Solway; and down the tide they shall everyone go, and well if we do not send a lessee along with them.'
>
> 'Friend,' replied Joshua, with a constrained smile, 'but that I know thou dost not mean as thou sayest, I would tell thee that we are under the protection of this country's laws; nor do we the less trust to obtain their protection, that our principles permit us not, by any act of violent resistance, to protect ourselves.'

'All villainous cant and cowardice,' exclaimed the fisherman, 'and assumed merely as a cloak to your hypocritical avarice.'

'Nay, say not cowardice, my friend,' answered the Quaker, 'since thou knowest there may be as much courage in enduring as in acting; and I will be judged by this youth, or by anyone else, whether there is no more cowardice – even in the opinion of that world whose thoughts are the breath in thy nostrils – in the armed oppressor who doth injury, than in the defenceless and patient sufferer who endureth it with constancy.'

In the character of Geddes we can see the passing of power from hereditary chieftains to new merchants. (The Quakers in the later eighteenth century had a growing reputation for piety and business.) Scott shows us that even in the small question of fishing-rights the old ways must be judged in relation to the changed and changing needs and conditions of the present. It is a sadder book than *Waverley* because these changes and changing needs are more clearly seen: 1763 is not 1745. We may note that the Quaker's ancestors behaved as Redgauntlet is behaving.

Yes, friend Latimer, my ancestors were renowned among the ravenous and bloodthirsty men who then dwelt in this vexed country; and so much were they famed for successful freebooting, robbery, and bloodshed that they are said to have been called Geddes, as likening them to the fish called a Jack, Pike, or Luce, and in our country tongue a Ged . . . (Letter 7)

Scott tells us that in some ways the two men were not unlike – both are 'blunt and unceremonious'. But the Quaker is the successful man; he has moved with the times, has the Law on his side, and knows that power lies there. And yet Scott, in this scene, keeps our sympathy for Redgauntlet – partly because in spite of the Quaker's piety it is Redgauntlet who is the simple man, and partly because we remember the glamour and sportsmanship of

Redgauntlet's fishing party – even though described by Darsie – and contrast the Quaker's way of fishing unfavourably with it. There is too much of Trumbull's 'all in the way of business' about it for our comfort. We do not like to see what is right coinciding so neatly with what is profitable.

A similar point is made in a very different way in the scene in chapter 16 where the Chevalier, under the name of Father Buonaventure, interviews Alan Fairford.

> 'Your name, sir, I am informed, is Fairford?' said the father. Alan answered by a bow.
>
> 'Called to the Scottish bar,' continued his visitor, 'There is, I believe, in the West, a family of birth and rank called Fairford of Fairford.'
>
> Alan thought this a strange observation from a foreign ecclesiastic, as his name intimated Father Buonaventure to be; but only answered, he believed there was such a family.
>
> 'Do you count kindred with them, Mr Fairford?' continued the inquirer.
>
> 'I have not the honour to lay such a claim,' said Fairford. 'My father's industry has raised his family from a low and obscure situation; I have no hereditary claim to distinction of any kind.'

It is the new men like Fairford (who represents the Law) and the Quaker (who represents Commerce) who will control Scotland, even though they have no 'hereditary claim' to do so. Once again Scott makes plain through his characters his awareness of those gradual changes in the society and economy of Scotland (changes still not completed in his own time) which leave no room for the older attitudes and ways of thinking and feeling, even when these ways have value. In this novel, as in *Persuasion*, 'The conflict is between the feudal remnant, conscious of its tradition, and the rising middle class, conscious of its vitality . . .'[2]

Scott respects Joshua Geddes and Alan Fairford; he admires them because they have, in their different ways, cut themselves off from the past and are living single-mindedly in the present and for the future; but he does not greatly like them. His deepest liking and sympathy are for Provost Crosbie, Pate-in-Peril, Nanty Ewart and Wandering Willie's 'gudesire', Steenie Steenson. A glance at one or two of these will suggest something of the organisation of the novel and how these characters (like Peter Peebles) are used to make a series of oblique comments on the theme. It is, in fact, in the organisation of these various comic characters that the essential structure of *Redgauntlet* is to be found.

Provost Crosbie, a Justice of the Peace, is a kind, canny, successful merchant who has some sympathy with the Jacobites, and not only because his wife is a forty-second cousin of Redgauntlet. He knows that the old days are gone and does not wish them back again. He knows, too, that their going has not been all gain (as Geddes and even Alan Fairford suggest), but that the decline in Jacobitism is a decline in the quality of living, a decline in moral standards or, at least, in fineness of feeling. And in chapter 10 when the provost talks to Alan (Crosbie takes up only two chapters in the book) all our regard is for Crosbie, with his greater warmth of human feeling and more sensitive evaluation of what has been lost. Crosbie is talking of another Jacobite, Pate-in-Peril:

> 'But though he is a windy body when he gets on his auld-warld stories, he has mair gumption in him than most people – knows business, Mr Alan, being bred to the law; but never took the gown because of the oaths, which kept more folk out then than they do now – the more's the pity.'
>
> 'What! Are you sorry, Provost, that Jacobitism is upon the decline?' said Fairford.

'No, no,' answered the Provost, 'I am only sorry for folks losing the tenderness of conscience which they used to have.'

We are invited to endorse Scott's approval of Crosbie because he combines something of the values of the older Scotland with a humane worldly-wisdom and a successful living in the present. He enjoys safety with honour. 'Wandering Willie's Tale' is too often regarded as being not only the best and only live part of the novel, but as easily (and luckily) detachable from it. For David Craig, Wandering Willie, along with Meg Merrilies (*Guy Mannering*) and Edie Ochiltree (*The Antiquary*), 'are none of them central to the drama of the novel. They wander around the main life, turning up when needed to pass off coincidences and surprises. What they are, of course, is vehicles for the author's "good Scots" and his miscellaneous lore.'[3] But the Tale is vital to *Redgauntlet*; it is a commentary – Scott's most brilliant comment – on the themes of the novel, and the comment is made through character – the character of Wandering Willie's father, Steenie Steenson. The Tale illustrates the common sense, vigour, courage and caution of Willie's 'gudesire'; it is through Scott's use of the earthy vernacular that we grasp these qualities as well as through the details of the story. It is often remarked that Scott's strength lies in his handling of the vernacular. What, perhaps, needs saying is that his strength lies here not simply because he had an ear for lowland speech, but because he endorsed those qualities of mind and character which the vernacular so accurately conveyed. In the vigorous flow of the Tale, Scott tells us something about courage, about honour and about the nature of the compromise that we must all make if we are to survive, as Steenie Steenson survives, great political changes with safety and honour. The tone of the Tale is similar to the tone of *Proud Maisie* – earthly, moral and savagely ironic. It is a hymn in praise of the unheroic, the reasonable and the sane. There is comment on 'great men':

> He was knighted at Lonon court, wi' the King's ain sword; and being a redhot prelatist, he came down here, rampauging like a lion, with commissions of lieutenancy (and of lunacy, for what I ken), to put down a' the Whigs and Covenanters in the country.

There is sharp knowledge of the ways of 'great men':

> The Whigs made an unca crawing what they wad do with their auld enemies, and in special wi' Sir Robert Redgauntlet. But there were ower mony great folks dipped in the same doings to make a spick and span new warld. So Parliament passed it a' ower easy; and Sir Robert, bating that he was held to hunting foxes instead of Covenanters, remained just the man he was.

And when Steenie visits hell to obtain his receipt there is condemnation of these ways:

> There was the Lang Lad of Nethertown, that helped to take Argyle; and the Bishop's summoner, that they called the Deil's Rattle-bag; and the wicked guardsmen, in their laced coats; and the savage Highland Amorites, that shed blood like water; and many a proud serving-man, haughty of heart and bloody of hand, cringing to the rich, and making them wickeder than they would be – grinding the poor to powder when the rich had broken them to fragments.

Steenie Steenson behaves with great courage in the story, not to gain honour, but to secure his receipt, and he lives successfully through a revolution (the older Redgauntlet in the story is a Jacobite, but his son is a Covenanter). The Tale is a sort of touchstone by which we are to judge Redgauntlet. It gives us our moral bearings and controls our reaction to the larger story. Steenie Steenson, like Provost Crosbie, is a successful man, and they both, suggests Scott, enjoy 'more safety, and even more honour' than Redgauntlet. The characters in *Redgauntlet* are all 'pointing not out or away from but directly at the very centre of the whole'.

'A strange delusion', says Darsie, on hearing from his sister Lilias in chapter 18 the full story of his uncle's attempts to restore the House of Stuart, 'and it is wonderful that it does not yield to the force of reality'. (In *Waverley* it was still possible to wonder, a very little, what the 'reality' was.) Darsie Latimer has been presented to us as an undistinguished and conventionally 'romantic' young man who early in the book has various delusions which gradually yield to the force of reality. He has found that 'romantic' situations are not, after all, so romantic when you are in them, and he would gladly escape to the safety of Edinburgh. Darsie falls in love with Lilias before he knows that she is his sister. This is his strangest delusion, and it is an episode which to many readers seems unsatisfactory and gratuitous. The unsatisfactoriness is there because Scott sentimentalises the predicament and its resolution. Darsie is not affected beyond feeling a temporary embarrassment; and this is sentimental because, as A. O. J. Cockshut has said, 'it evades the natural consequences of the plot – the inevitable psychological disturbance which would occur when a man found that the woman he loved was really his sister'.[4] Incest was nothing new in English fiction. Miss Tompkins writes:

one notes the extraordinary pervasiveness through all grades of the novel of the theme of incest. The notorious *Morning Ramble* began with a double suggestion of incest, averted, as is so often the case, by the discovery that some jugglery has been practised with babes in cradles. This was the way of Fletcher in *A King and No King*, and a disingenuous way it is. Careless nurses, gypsies, unacknowledged marriages, changes of name, – all these devices are used to introduce the theme of incestuous love, and used again to avert the tragedy and unite the lovers. The novelists perpetually hover round the subject; they refer to it by suggestion to enrich the heroine's distress, even if it forms no part of the plot proper, and the persecuting lover, who is most distasteful to her, frequently turns out to be her near relative . . .

The theme has been so closely associated with romantic and revolutionary poets that its wide dispersion in the 'seventies and 'eighties, a generation before the master utterances of romantic poetry, is worthy of note. It was perhaps one of the many signs of that blind craving for the passionate and extraordinary, which the calm façade of eighteenth-century literature had never wholly concealed, and which now became from year to year more conspicuous. The romantic poets did not reintroduce the theme; they found it, in the first place, in the novels that they devoured as boys. What they did was to make it painfully real, and after that it was not long before public taste turned against it.[5]

In *Redgauntlet* Darsie's love for his sister may or may not be part of the 'plot proper', but it is part of the novel proper. Scott makes a conventional device of fiction a part of the novel's structure. For the point of the episode is clear. Darsie's delusion has to yield to reality as all other delusions in the book have to yield to reality, however dull that reality may be and however attractive the delusions. If Scott's handling of the incest theme remains unsatisfactory it is because the scene is never 'painfully real'; but Darsie's discovery that Greenmantle is his sister makes it easier for him to resist his uncle's plans to involve him in rebellion.

In the final scene (chapters 20 to 23), which follows close on Darsie's discovery that Lilias is his sister, Scott again insists that life is relentlessly humdrum, with no place for nostalgia or simple heroics or large gestures. As the action unfolds in Joe Crackenthorp's public-house, we are moved by the sight of Redgauntlet's strange delusion being destroyed by anti-climax – by one unarmed man, General Campbell, and his promise to make no arrests if all the conspirators, including the Chevalier, will quietly depart. The reluctant Jacobites are unable to decide what to do.

Amid this scene of confusion, a gentleman, plainly dressed in a riding-habit, with a black cockade in his hat, but without any arms except a *couteau-de-chasse*, walked into the apartment without ceremony. He was a tall, thin, gentlemanly man, with a look and bearing decidedly military. He had passed through their guards, if in the confusion they now maintained any, without stop or question, and now stood, almost unarmed, among armed men, who, nevertheless gazed on him as on the angel of destruction.

General Campbell, after some extravagant gestures from Prince Charles Edward and the more loyal Jacobites, speaks to them all:

'Exaggerated accounts of your purpose have been laid before government by the information of a traitor in your own counsels; and I was sent down post to take the command of a sufficient number of troops, in case these calumnies should be found to have any real foundation. I have come here, of course, sufficiently supported both with cavalry and infantry to do whatever might be necessary; but my commands are – and I am sure they agree with my inclination – to make no arrests, nay, to make no further inquiries of any kind, if this good assembly will consider their own interest so far as to give up their own immediate purpose, and return quietly home to their own houses.'

'What! – all?' exclaimed Sir Richard Glendale – 'all, without exception?'

'ALL, without one single exception,' said the General; 'such are my orders. If you accept my terms, say so, and make haste; for things may happen to interfere with his Majesty's kind purposes towards you all.'

AW E

'His Majesty's kind purposes!' said the Wanderer [Prince Charles Edward]. 'Do I hear you aright, sir?'

'I speak the King's very words, from his very lips,' replied the General ... 'His Majesty will not even believe that the most zealous Jacobites who yet remain can nourish a thought of exciting a civil war, which must be fatal to their families and themselves, besides spreading bloodshed and ruin through a peaceful land ...'

'Is this real?' said Redgauntlet. 'Can you mean this? Am I – are all – are any of these gentlemen at liberty, without interruption, to embark in yonder brig, which, I see, is now again approaching the shore?'

'You, sir – all – any of the gentlemen present,' said the General – 'all whom the vessel can contain, are at liberty to embark, uninterrupted by me; but I advise none to go off who have not powerful reasons unconnected with the present meeting, for this will be remembered against no one.'

'Then, gentlemen,' said Redgauntlet, clasping his hands together as the words burst from him, 'the cause is lost for ever!'

It is the finest climax in Scott's novels; and how completely the success of the scene depends on, results from and clinches everything in the book before it can be gauged by comparing it with a similar scene at the end of *The Black Dwarf*. In that novel, which tells of an attempted Jacobite rising in 1709, the hero Hobbie Elliot surprises the Jacobites, already in some disarray, and speaks to them and dissolves their attempt very much as General Campbell does in Redgauntlet:

'By Heaven! it is true, Sir Frederick; the house is filled with armed men, and our drunken beasts are all disarmed. – Draw, and let us fight our way.'

'Binna rash – binna rash,' exclaimed Hobbie; 'hear me a bit, hear me a bit. We mean ye nae harm; but, as ye are in arms for King James, as ye ca' him, and the prelates, we thought it right to keep up the auld neighbour war, and stand up for the t'other ane and the Kirk; but we'll no hurt a hair o' your heads, if ye like to gang hame quietly . . . '(ch. 17)

If this is unimpressive and lacks the resonance of the other scene it is because it has no place in the narrative structure of the novel; it has not been worked for in all that has gone before. The climax of *Redgauntlet* is an episode of Scott's fine artistic tact – his firm Augustan grasp of social realities – that Redgauntlet should not be destroyed by military action (he is denied a heroic death) because military action (and heroic deaths) have been shown in the novel to be irrelevant in the changed times since 1745. You cannot put back the clock (the curse on the House of Redgauntlet is that it has always tried to do this), and we feel that Redgauntlet has been defeated by something more formidable than force of arms – the passage of time. 'The cause is lost forever', exclaims Redgauntlet (we recognise that 'the cause' is something much finer and larger than a political loyalty), and it and he are lost because they are now anachronisms.

Redgauntlet stands alone at the end – splendid, heroic, courageous, romantic and absurd. Scott's triumph in the final scene – and he has worked for it throughout the book – is his success in so controlling and directing our feelings that we share his firm and complex attitude to Redgauntlet. We don't think of Scott as a symbolic writer, but some of the force of the last scene comes from Scott's use of his characters as symbols. The final desperate discussions of the Jacobites, and the negotiations with General Campbell, are not conducted on their own. In *Waverley* our uninterrupted attention was given to the trial and execution of Vich Ian Vohr and Evan Maccombich. But here Geddes and Fairford intrude and hinder the action; Redgauntlet has to try to quieten them and is then obliged to lock them up. This small hindrance is appropriately significant of the larger meaning, that it is, indeed, the new middle-class Scotland, it is the Law and the changing social and economic patterns as represented by the Quaker and Alan Fairford that have put paid to the older way of life. The social comment is achieved through character; the lesson is driven home simply because Geddes and Alan are there. And Peter Peebles is there, too, in the last scene with something of the force of a symbolic character, Folly, to act as Scott's final ironic and compassionate comment on the action of the novel. In chapter 23 he talks about his protracted lawsuit to Joshua Geddes:

> 'It's very true that it is grandeur upon earth to hear one's name thunnered out along the long-arched roof of the Outer House, – '*Poor* Peter Peebles against Plainstanes, *et per contra*; a' the best lawyers in the house fleeing like eagles to the prey, some because they are in the cause, and some because they want to be thought engaged (for there are tricks in other trades by selling muslins) – to see the reporters mending their pens to take down the debate – the Lords themselves pooin' in their chairs, like folk sitting down to a gude dinner, and crying on the clerks for parts and pendicles of the process, who, puir bodies, can do little mair than cry on their closet-keepers to help them. To see a' this,' continued Peter, in a tone of sustained rapture, 'and to ken that naething will be said or dung amang a' these grand folk, for maybe the feck of three hours, saying what concerns you and your business – oh, man, nae wonder that ye judge this to be earthly glory! And yet, neighbour, as I was saying, there be unco drawbacks. I whiles think of my bit house, where dinner, and supper, and breakfast used to come without the crying for, just as if fairies had brought it – and the gude bed at e'en – and the needfu' penny in the pouch. And then to see a' anes warldly substance capering in the air in a pair of weigh-bauks, now up, now down, as the breath of judge or counsel inclines it for pursuer or defender. Troth, man, there are times I rue having ever begun the plea wark – though, maybe, when ye consider

the renown and credit I have by it, ye will hardly believe what I am saying.'

'Indeed, friend,' said Joshua, with a sigh, 'I am glad thou hast found anything in the legal contention which compensates thee for poverty and hunger; but I believe, were other human objects of ambition looked upon as closely, their advantages would be found as chimerical as those attending thy protracted litigation.'

We scarcely need the Quaker's moralising comment to recognise that Scott achieves something of his valuable complexity of feelings towards Redgauntlet (who, after all, stands for much that Scott loved and admired) by relating his affairs with those of Peter Peebles, and the 'sustained rapture' of their talk, and their futile committing of all their 'warldly substance'.

Notes

CHAPTER ONE
(pages 11–33)

1 J. G. Lockhart, *Life of Scott*, ch. 35.
2 *Miscellaneous Prose Works* (Edinburgh, 1848) III 409.
3 *The Letters of Sir Walter Scott, 1787–1807*, ed. H. J. C. Grierson (1932) p. 265.
4 *Miscellaneous Prose Works*, III 296.
5 *Quarterly Review*, XIV (1815) 189.
6 *Miscellaneous Prose Works*, III 359–60.
7 Ibid. III 173.
8 Ibid. III 462.
9 Ibid. III 403.
10 Ibid. III 413.
11 Ibid. IV 10–14.
12 Introduction to *The Monastery*.
13 *Miscellaneous Prose Works*, IV 66.
14 Mary Lascelles, 'Scott and the Art of Revision', in *Imagined Worlds*, ed. Maynard Mack and Ian Gregor (1968) p. 152.
15 *Journal* (Edinburgh, 1927) pp. 103–4.
16 *Miscellaneous Prose Works*, XVIII 200.
17 Ibid. XVIII 291–2.
18 Ibid. III 376.
19 Ibid. III 371 n.
20 Ibid. III 372.3.
21 Ibid. III 388.
22 Ibid. III 388.
23 Lockhart, ch. 59.
24 Francis R. Hart, *Scott's Novels* (Charlottesville, 1966) p. 22.
25 George Watson (ed.) *Castle Rackrent* (1964) p. vii.
26 Ibid. p. x.
27 Ibid. pp. 4–5.
28 *Castle Rackrent*, ed. Bruce Teets (University of Miami Press, 1964) p. 28.

29 Watson, op. cit. p. xvii.
30 Hart, op. cit. p. 337.
31 Roger McHugh, 'Maria Edgeworth's Irish Novels', in *Studies*, XXVII (1938) 568.

CHAPTER TWO

(pages 34–55)

1   Carlyle, 'Sir Walter Scott', in *Critical and Miscellaneous Essays*, III 214.
2   G. M. Young, 'Scott and the Historians', in *Sir Walter Scott Lectures, 1940–1948*, ed. W. L. Renwick (Edinburgh, 1950) p. 98.
3   Ibid. p. 104.
4   Sir Herbert Grierson, 'History and the Novel', in *Sir Walter Scott Lectures, 1940–1948*, ed. Renwick, p. 45.
5   H. Butterfield, *The Historical Novel* (Cambridge, 1924) p. 36.
6   Georg Lukács, *The Historical Novel*, tr. H. and S. Mitchell (1962) p. 42.
7   Butterfield, op. cit. p. 55.
8   Ibid. p. 50.
9   Thomas Crawford, *Scott* (Edinburgh, 1965) p. 50.
10 Donald Davie, *The Heyday of Sir Walter Scott* (1961) p. 26.
11 Johnson, *The Rambler*, no. 151.
12 Davie, op. cit. p. 26.
13 Alexander Welsh, *The Hero of the Waverley Novels* (New Haven and London, 1963) p. 87.
14 Leslie Stephen, 'Some Words about Sir Walter Scott', in *Hours in a Library* (First Series).
15 Lukács, op. cit. p. 35.
16 Arnold Kettle, *An Introduction to the English Novel* (1951) I 115.
17 Lukács, op. cit. p. 58.
18 R. G. Collingwood, *The Idea of History* (Oxford, 1946) p. 123.
19 Francis R. Hart, *Scott's Novels* (Charlottesville, 1966) p. 182.
20 Davie, op. cit. p. 62.
21 *Joseph Andrews*, bk III, ch. 1.
22 J. H. Raleigh, 'What Scott meant to the Victorians', in *Victorian Studies*, vol. VII, no. 1 (1963) 23.
23 David Daiches, 'Scott's achievement as a Novelist', in *Literary Essays* (Edinburgh and London, 1956) p. 119.

24   Lukács, op. cit. p. 32.
25   *Waverley*, ch. 72.
26   Hart, op. cit. pp. 337–8.
27   Ibid. p. 338.
28   Daiches, op. cit. pp. 92–3.
29   *Coleridge's Miscellaneous Criticism*, ed. T. M. Raysor (1936) pp. 341–2.
30   Welsh, op. cit. p. 57.
31   Daiches, op. cit. p. 96.

CHAPTER THREE
(pages 56–80)

1   Scott reviewed *Tales of My Landlord* (First Series), i.e. *Old Mortality* and *The Black Dwarf*, in order to convince the world in general and John Murray in particular that he was not 'The Author of Waverley'. Scott wrote to Murray on 18 December 1916 and said: 'I assure you I have never read a volume of them [*Tales of My Landlord*] till they were printed . . . I do not expect implicit reliance to be placed on my disavowal . . . But I have a mode of convincing you that I am perfectly serious in my denial . . . and that is, by reviewing the work . . .'

2   *Quarterly Review*, xvi (1817) 431.

3   John Holloway, *The Charted Mirror* (1960) p. 106.

4   J. M. S. Tompkins, *The Popular Novel in England, 1770–1800* (1932) p. 344.

5   John Adolphus, *Letters to Richard Heber*, 2nd ed. (Edinburgh, 1822) pp. 192–3.

6   *Edinburgh Review*, xxiv (1815) 208.

7   J. G. Lockhart, *Life of Scott*, ch. 33.

8   In no other of Scott's novels is the passivity of the hero more marked. This passivity is noted by Scott in the passage from the *Quarterly Review* quoted at the beginning of this chapter. For a full discussion of this topic see Alexander Welsh, *The Hero of the Waverley Novels* (New Haven, 1963) ch. 2.

9   W. P. Ker, *On Modern Literature* (Oxford, 1955) p. 108.

10   Donald Davie, *The Heyday of Sir Walter Scott* (1961) p. 33.

11   'For example, we are told that he could imagine no subject so perfectly suited for fiction as the 'Forty-five. Yet that event was surely more of an outbreak or flare-up, which passed off without seriously

affecting Scott's society, than something fundamental in his past. We can see that he, in particular, would be bound to seize on the 'Forty-five for its possibilities as a glamorous romance (the last flourish of the tartan).' David Craig, *Scottish Literature and the Scottish People, 1680–1830* (1961) p. 152.

12 'the elegiac is often accompanied by a diffused, resigned melancholy sense of the passing of time, of the old order changing and yielding to a new one'. Northrop Frye, *Anatomy of Criticism* (Princeton, 1957) p. 36.

13 Ibid. p. 36.

14 S. Stewart Gordon, '*Waverley* and the "Unified Design"', in *Journal of English Literary History*, xviii (1951) 107–22.

15 *Quarterly Review*, xi (1814) 356.

16 *Quarterly Review*, xvi (1817) 432.

17 For an excellent discussion of the notion of 'Honour' in the Waverley novels see Alexander Welsh, *The Hero in the Waverley Novels* (New Haven and London, 1963) ch. 8. Of particular interest is his remark: 'The Waverley Novels, like the contemporary arguments against duelling, insist that honour must no longer lead to homicide.' Welsh traces the notorious passivity of Scott's heroes to the notion of Honour that Scott himself accepted.

18 For E. M. W. Tillyard the Baron is very close to the Trojans in *Troilus and Cressida*. See *Shakespeare's Problem Plays* (1950) p. 59.

19 Lockhart, *Life of Scott*, ch. 27.

CHAPTER FOUR
(pages 81–98)

1 John Adolphus, *Letters to Richard Heber*, 2nd ed. (Edinburgh, 1822) p. 14.

2 A. R. Humphreys (ed.) *Henry IV (part i)* (London 1960) p. liv.

3 Ibid. p. xliii.

4 Donald Davie, *The Heyday of Sir Walter Scott* (1961) p. 62.

5 Ibid. pp. 61–2.

6 Ibid. p. 63. Dr Craig makes the same point: 'Fairservice is not a significant force in the drama, he is just Scott's kind of light relief criticised by Coleridge: "One most characteristic quality of Sir Walter Scott's novels is the charm and yet the utterly impersonal and undramatic stuff of the dialogues."' *Scottish Literature and the Scottish People, 1680–1830*, p. 180.

7 Davie, op. cit. p. 64.
8 Alexander Welsh, *The Hero in the Waverley Novels* (New Haven, 1963) pp. 188–9.

CHAPTER FIVE
(pages 99–113)

1 John Adolphus, *Letters to Richard Heber*, 2nd ed. (Edinburgh, 1922) p. 14.
2 Lockhart, *Life of Scott*, ch. 48.
3 Georg Lukács, *The Historical Novel*, tr. H. and S. Mitchell (1962) p. 35.
4 Adolphus, op. cit. p. 14.
5 Ibid. p. 15.
6 The novel properly begins in chapter 2. The first chapter is concerned with editorial matter.
7 I use the word 'house' (as Scott does) in the senses of 'family' and 'dwelling-place'. In the novel Scott continually parallels the fate of the house of Ravenswood with the crumbling condition of Wolf's Crag. In the final chapter Ravenswood refers to himself as a 'falling tower'; and there is obvious symbolism in chapter 10, when Ravenswood and Lucy meet for the first time in a fierce storm: 'the storm-cloud was very near the castle; and the peal was so sudden and dreadful that the old tower rocked to its foundation'.
8 There is little point in discussing whether Caleb is an 'overripe character', as David Craig calls him. The point about Caleb is that he superbly fulfils a narrative function in the novel.
9 Lukács, op. cit. p. 49.
10 Ibid. p. 34.

CHAPTER SIX
(pages 114–33)

1 Hereditary, or inherited, jurisdiction was the exercise of judicial authority, or of the functions of a judge or legal tribunal, by certain Scottish nobles and clan leaders, who succeeded to these rights by inheritance. The Act of Union (1707) had guaranteed these rights, and when they were abolished compensation was paid.
2 Marvin Mudrick, *Jane Austen*, p. 232.

3   David Craig, *Scottish Literature and the Scottish People, 1680–1830*
    (1961) pp. 150–1.

4   A. O. J. Cockshut, *The Twentieth Century*, CLXI (1957) 361.

5   J. M. S. Tompkins, *The Popular Novel in England, 1770–1800*
    (1932) pp. 62–6.

Index

Adolphus, John 59, 81, 101–2
Aristotle 36
Austen, Jane
   Mansfield Park 62
   Persuasion 123

Bage, Robert 17
Ballantyne, James 23
Blackwood's Edinburgh Magazine
   24

Calprenède 15
Carlyle, Thomas 34
Cockshut, A. O. J. 127
Coleridge, S. T. 52–3
Craig, David 69, 125

Daiches, David 52, 54, 92–3,
   94–5
Davie, Donald 38, 40, 69, 97

Edgeworth, Maria 29–33
   The Absentee 32
   Castle Rackrent 31, 32
Edinburgh Review 82

Fielding, Henry 21, 23, 39
   Joseph Andrews 47
   Tom Jones 21, 23
Fletcher, John 29
Frye, Northrop 70

Goldsmith, Oliver 14
   The Vicar of Wakefield 14
Grierson, H. J. C. 36, 38

Hart, Francis R, 31
Hegel 45

Jeffrey, Francis 12
Johnson, Samuel 12, 14, 23

Ker, W. P. 66
Kettle, Arnold 44

Lascelles, Mary 23
Le Sage 19
   Le Diable Boiteux 19
   Gil Blas 19, 20
Lockhart, J. G. 30, 99
Lukács, Georg 44–5, 46

MacKenzie, Henry 19–20, 24
   The Man of Feeling 19–20, 58
Marx, Karl 45
Muir, Kenneth 82

Quarterly Review 56, 73

Radcliffe, Ann 15–16, 23, 26,
   27, 29
Richardson, Samuel 13, 22–3

Scott, Walter
   The Abbot 21, 36
   The Antiquary 17, 26
   The Black Dwarf 130–1
   The Bride of Lammermoor 28,
      35, 49, 96, 99–113
   Chronicles of the Canongate
      42–3

Scott, Walter—*contd.*
 The Fair Maid of Perth 32, 44
 The Fortunes of Nigel 18–19,
   44
 The Highland Widow 49–52
 Ivanhoe 35, 38, 40–1
 A Legend of Montrose 19, 54,
   81–90
 Letters on Demonology and
   Witchcraft 27
 The Monastery 14, 23, 25, 43
 Old Mortality 19, 86
 Quentin Durward 42
 Redgauntlet 32, 43, 47, 54,
   82, 85, 86, 100, 101, 103,
   114–33
 Rob Roy 19, 45, 47, 86, 90–8
 St Ronan's Well 32
 Tales of My Landlord 56
 Wandering Willie's Tale 23,
   28, 54, 125–7
 Waverley 12, 17, 19, 30–1, 32,
   35, 38, 39–40, 43, 45, 56–

   80, 86, 103, 114–15, 116–
   117
 Woodstock 23–4
Scudéry, Madeleine de 15
Shakespeare 27, 73, 96
Shelley, Mary
 Frankenstein 23, 24, 25–6
Smith, Charlotte 21
Smollett, Tobias 17
 Roderick Random 20
Sterne, Laurence 20
 A Sentimental Journey 58
 Tristram Shandy 14

Tompkins, J. M. S. 58, 127

Walpole, Horace 27
 The Castle of Otranto 23, 24
Watson, George 31, 32
Welsh, Alexander 41, 66, 97–8,
   108

Young, G. M. 34–5

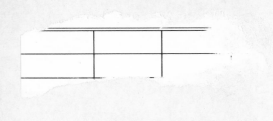